The Art of
Letter-Writing

The Art of Letter-Writing

HOW TO ADDRESS
EVERY OCCASION

GEORGINA HARRIS

CICO BOOKS

LONDON NEW YORK

Dedication
Maiken—beautiful inside and out
(like all the best letters)

Published in 2009 by CICO Books
An imprint of
Ryland Peters & Small
20–21 Jockey's Fields   519 Broadway, 5th Floor
London WC1R 4BW   New York, NY 10012

www.cicobooks.com

10 9 8 7 6 5 4 3 2 1

A CIP catalog record for this book is available from the Library of Congress
and the British Library.

ISBN-13: 978 1 906525 83 5

Printed in China

Design: David Fordham
Illustration: Michael A Hill

contents

introduction

A really good letter is one of life's small but enduring joys—from the promise of a fat, creamy envelope to the messages of fun, love, and warmth that it holds within it, letters deserve their reputation as important parts of ourselves and our lives. Whether you want to announce a great life event, declare your love, or thank a beloved friend, letters are practical magic.

The secret to creating a good letter is simple, and if you use this book, probably foolproof. Each chapter provides the right wording for you to use for all life occasions—you only need to add names and personal details. Clear sections lay out the right forms, correct wording, and clear phrasing that communicates your message well and respects you and your reader. Templates, tips, and examples show you step by step how to create invitations for life events, including weddings, Bar Mitzvahs, and birthday parties.

Many people now believe that good manners can never be underrated as a life skill: a good letter is about honoring yourself and others, and there is nothing trivial about that. This book shows you how to behave perfectly—in writing—and how to maximize the delight of a great correspondence to you and your recipient.

Yet letters are not all about correct form; expressing love, joy, and even sadness and loss are vital too. Love letters, thank-you letters, and bereavement letters are covered here too—with step-by-step ways that help you to negotiate and release the delicate world of inner feeling that sometimes seems hard to us all. The book shows you how to express yourself and gives tips that will trigger your own creative power to create truly personal, moving, and memorable writing.

But not every letter we need to write is social or personal—we all need to get vital messages across in the world of work and business. The book tells you how to write letters that get results. Facing the heart-sinking task of a letter of complaint? Need your money back? You will learn how to get your message across with maximum elegance and élan. The templates provided in this book show you how to negotiate the 21st century, with its reams of electronic and business communication, and explain the new rules of netiquette.

Both practical and personal, if you follow the guidelines here, you will acquire the power of social and emotional chic—a life skill not to be underrated, and one of the most delightful and rewarding you and all those in your world can enjoy.

CHAPTER 1

Invitations and Announcements

There are always occasions in life when you need to send invitations, and handwritten invitations are always appreciated. This chapter looks at various events, from weddings and christenings to birthday and anniversary parties, and shows you the best way to write to your guests.

A WEDDING
preparing for the big day

Just as you might choose a white gown and update it in a fashionable cut, so the stylish modern bride needs chic invitations, too—classic, correct, elegant, and modern. This section shows you how to write invitations that stand up smartly to the severest matters of etiquette, and all their many intricate customs, yet allows you the flexibility to introduce individual touches to make the invitations your own.

how to get it right

Without doubt our most important social celebration today, the wedding is a time for whole-hearted enjoyment. More than just a marriage, the festivities usually involve at least two families, a huge crowd of friends, and much affection and laughter, as well as the passion of two people in love. Tradition is vital; just as the age-old customs of the white dress and enormous cake have stayed with us, so have the rituals and wording of the nuptial announcements and invitations.

Using courteous invitation etiquette shows you are treating all your guests with value, and lays the foundation for a memorable and glorious wedding. Using the tried-and-tested techniques outlined in the examples below, you can elegantly sidestep any of the little glitches in "form" that can cause such startling fireworks among your loved ones, and set up a day that everyone will remember with joy.

In addition to the invitation itself, you will find yourself with a welter of announcements, cards, and other correspondence to deal with. Everything should be done in a style complementary to the main invitation, and hints and tips are included here to show you how.

how to announce your engagement

There is no need to mail formal announcements of an engagement or a betrothal. Apart from anything else, every recipient would expect an invitation to your wedding, which may not suit your plans, and you may feel pressured into fixing a date and a list a little prematurely.

A newspaper announcement is easier, less costly, and surprisingly effective, particularly now that major newspapers will also put your announcement online. *The New York Times*, *The Times*, and the *Daily Telegraph* all carry daily listings. You can find each publication's submission guidelines, deadlines, (modest) fees, and regulations online.

For an engagement announcement, the wording is as follows:

Mr S White and Miss E D Dean
The engagement is announced between Scott Archibald,
son of Mr and Mrs Tom White of Loughborough, Yorkshire,
and Elizabeth Davina, elder daughter of Mr and Mrs David Dean,
of Bristol, Avon.

If you wish to set a date for the wedding, why not include it? Your announcement can double as a Save the Date card (see page 12).

Unlike a wedding date, which should be announced to all when you become engaged, you should start by telling your nearest and dearest in this order: children; parents; grandparents; brothers and sisters; other close relatives; friends; your boss and colleagues.

Or, why not throw an engagement party? It's much more fun and more of a celebration than leaving messages on all of your busy friends' cell phones.

save the date card

Once you have reserved the big day, you may also wish to reserve your guests. A Save the Date card allows you to make sure your most precious friends and family are able to attend, and gives you a handy idea of guest numbers.
Choose one of these forms:

SAVE THE DATE

Flora Finch
and Fred Sparrow
are getting married
Please save the date of
their wedding
May 1, 2010
Invitation to follow

SAVE THE DATE

We are delighted to
announce
That we will be getting
married on
May 1, 2010
Invitation to follow
Flora Finch
and Fred Sparrow

SAVE THE DATE

May 1, 2010
Flora Finch and Fred Sparrow's
Wedding
Invitation to follow

SAVE THE DATE

May 1, 2010
is our wedding day
and we would like
you to join us
Flora and Fred
Invitation to follow

wedding shower etiquette

Luckily, this is one task that the bride or her family has no part in; your chief bridesmaid, maid of honor, or closest girlfriend, will act as hostess. The bride should be asked for her guest list, then others will plan and host the bridal shower. Including gift lists or store registry information on a separate sheet is helpful to all. Brides can then write thank-you notes for their shower gifts (see page 92).

the wedding invitation

For centuries, the custom stood for engagement announcements and wedding invitations to be sent by the bride's parents. Nowadays, thanks to the extended family (and, for most people, the cost of the ceremonies), it has become increasingly common for both sets of parents, or the bride and groom, to fund the wedding. The rule here is that whoever pays is the host, and therefore sends, and receives replies to, all of the invitations.

If costs are being shared, the names of both sets of parents can appear at the top of the invitation—the bride's before the groom's.

Nowadays, most couples share a large proportion of the wedding costs and if so, they may host the wedding with or without naming their parents on the invitation.

Increasingly, you have the choice of two types of perfectly correct invitation—one with more formal wording than the other. A less formal invitation usually has the words: **"would like you to join"** instead of **"request the pleasure of your company"** and may, for example, state in full: **"The reception afterwards will be at..."** rather than just naming the venue.

the seven golden rules of wedding invitations

1. A formal wedding invitation—on card or paper—is still a must. Avoid email or "e-vites."
2. Be clear about whether you are inviting the guests' children or babies.
3. If boy- or girlfriends are invited, name them as often as you can. "Plus one" can be tactful for your more romantically active friends, but may seem a little careless.

4. Avoid mentioning wedding gifts on the invitation—include a slip in the envelope.
5. If you are holding a daytime ceremony with a dance afterwards, include a dress code.
6. Send out all the invitations at the same time. No one likes feeling B-list.
7. As a rule, about a quarter of guests will decline; your guest list can reflect this.

FORMAL WEDDING INVITATION

The classic Anglophile invitation has formal wording, which is sent to all guests.

FORMAL INVITATION
The bride's parents should use this style of invitation for a daytime wedding.

[name of guests in handwriting]

Mr and Mrs *[husband's first name and surname of bride's parents]*

request the pleasure of your company
at the marriage of their daughter
[first name of bride]

to Mr *[groom's first name and surname]*

at
[ceremony venue, not with address]
on
[day of week, month, day, time—do not include year]
and afterwards at
[name of reception venue, no address]

RSVP
[include phone number/email address]

Wedding Invitation Variations

Although the invitation on page 17 is the classic style, there are cases in which a different version is needed, due to family circumstances or simply a desire for a less formal approach. The variations on these pages allow for this and can be adapted as necessary.

LESS FORMAL INVITATION
Many people nowadays prefer to use this version of the invitation.

Mr and Mrs [husband's first name and surname of bride's parents]
request the honor of the presence of
Mr and Mrs [guests by name]
at the marriage of their daughter
[first name of bride]
to
Mr [first name and family name]
on [day of week, month, day—not year]
at [time of day and name of ceremony location]

and afterwards at
[reception location, not full address]

RSVP
[bride's mother only]
[include phone number/email address]

Mr and Mrs *[husband's first name and surname of bride's parents]*
would like
[first name of guests]
to join them to celebrate
the marriage of their daughter
[first name of bride]
and
Mr *[first name and family name]*
[day of week, month, day——not year]
at *[time of day and ceremony venue with address]*

and afterwards for a party at
[reception location and full address]

RSVP
[include phone number / email address]

INFORMAL INVITATION
Another more informal approach that the bride's parents can use.

INVITATION FOR DIVORCED PARENTS
If the bride's parents are divorced, and her mother has yet to marry again, use this style.

Mrs *[mother's first name and surname]*
and Mr *[father's first name and surname]*
request the honor of the presence of
Mr and Mrs *[guests by name]*
at the marriage of their daughter
[first name of bride]
to
Mr *[first name and family name]*

[day of week, month, day——not year]
at *[time of day and name of ceremony venue]*

and afterwards at
[reception location, not full address]

RSVP
[include phone number / email address]

INVITATION FOR MOTHER AND STEPFATHER

This can be used if the mother and stepfather are hosting the event. If the divorced father and (not remarried) mother are hosts, start with the father's first name and surname and the mother's first name and surname.

Mr and Mrs *[stepfather's first name and surname]*

request the pleasure of your company at the marriage of her daughter
[bride's first name and surname]
to
Mr *[groom's first name and surname]*

at *[ceremony venue, not with address]*
on *[day of week, month, day, time—not year]*

and afterwards at
[reception location, no address]

RSVP
[include phone number/email address]

Miss *[bride's first name and surname]*
and
Mr *[groom's first name and surname]*

request the honor of the presence of
Mr and Mrs *[guests by name]*
at their marriage on
[day of week, month, day—not year]
at *[time of day and name of ceremony venue]*

and afterwards at
[reception location, not full address]

RSVP
[bride's mother—only]
[include phone number/email address]

FORMAL INVITATION VARIATION

If the happy couple are hosting their own wedding, this form can be used.

"This is the day we celebrate the joys of today, the memories of yesterday, and the hopes of tomorrow."

ANONYMOUS

WEDDING RECEPTION INVITATIONS

As many weddings go on for nearly 24 hours now, you may want to issue a separate invitation to a dinner and/or dancing afterwards. In this case, it is acceptable to add "Dinner and Dancing (by separate invitation) at 7.30pm" to the wedding invitation and to enclose a separate card of invitation to the evening reception. You may wish to send a more informal invitation; in order to do this, simply alter the wording of the formal invitation below to: "Mr and Mrs Sam Smith would like Mr and Mrs [husband's first name and surname] to join them at the evening reception celebrating the marriage of their daughter...." The address of the reception venue could also be included.

Mr and Mrs [husband's first name and surname of bride's parents]
request the pleasure of the company of
Mr and Mrs [guests by name]

at a reception
to celebrate the marriage of their daughter

[first name of bride]
to
Mr [first name and family name]

on [day of week, month, day—not year]
at [time of day and name of reception location, not full address]

RSVP
[include phone number/email address]

FORMAL INVITATION
The classic style for a wedding reception invitation.

VARIATION ON THE FORMAL INVITATION
This style can be used when only a few guests are invited to the actual wedding ceremony.

Mr and Mrs [husband's first name and surname of bride's parents]

request the pleasure of your company
at a reception following the marriage of

[first name of bride]
to
Mr [groom's first name and surname]

at [name of reception venue, no address]

on [day of week, month, day, and time—do not include year]

RSVP
[include phone number/email address]

INVITATION FOR A LATER RECEPTION
Style to use for a reception which takes place at a later date, for example, after the honeymoon.

Mr and Mrs [husband's first name and surname of bride's parents]
request the pleasure of your company

at a reception to celebrate the marriage of

[first name of bride]
to
Mr [groom's first name and surname]

at [name of reception venue, no address]

on [day of week, month, day, and time—do not include year]

RSVP
[include phone number/email address]

jewish wedding invitation

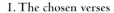

Traditionally a work of beauty and poetry, a Jewish wedding invitation always includes verses celebrating the nuptials. Also customary are personalized invitations, possibly in Hebrew, and response cards. The order of text includes:

1. The chosen verses
2. Full name of bride
3. Full name of bridegroom
4. Name and address of the house of worship
5. Address of the reception
6. Date and time of both the ceremony and the reception
7. Whether there is to be a kiddush after the service
8. The signature(s) of the host or hosts, if any
9. RSVP details (in addition to the response card you have provided)

verses for the jewish wedding invitation

Use one of these verses in your invitation:

"I will betroth you unto me forever,
in justice, in righteousness,
in loving kindness, in compassion,
and in faith."
The words form a circle, like the ring on my finger,
without beginning or end.

From generation to generation
We carry on
With the richness of tradition
And the promise of tomorrow.

Grant us long life,
A life of peace,
A life of goodness,
A life of blessing,
A life of strength and health,
A life of piety,
A life free of shame and reproach,
A life of wealth and honor,
A life full of love of Torah and fear of the Heavens
A life in which all our hearts' desires for goodness
Will be fulfilled.

addressing the guests

Envelopes are always to be addressed formally, whether for wedding invitations or for more personal correspondence. (Even if the letter inside begins, "Heads-up, Sweetcheeks," the recipient should be named with their proper title—such as "TDN Whitney, Chairman, Megacorp Industries." The principle here is that, just as you wouldn't call a lover a secret name at a social gathering, so you honor the divide between public and personal life.)

The list below gives correct titles, depending on your recipient's social status.

ladies:

Single lady who is unmarried or cohabiting—**Miss or Ms Jane Johnson**
Married lady—**Mrs John Williams**
Married lady who uses own surname—**Mrs Jane Johnson and John Williams, Esq.**
Divorced lady—**Mrs Jane Johnson**
Widowed lady—**Mrs Samuel Smith**

couples:

Married couple—**Mr and Mrs John Wiliams**
Cohabiting couple—**Miss Jane Johnson and Mr Mark Mitchell**
Married doctors—**The Doctors Gonzalez**
Doctor wife—**Dr June Gonzalez and Mr Juan Gonzalez**
Doctor husband—**Dr and Mrs John Jones**

friends living together:

Miss Kate Brown and Miss Lola Lopez
Mr David Davis and Mr Frank Field
Who goes first? Generally, the oldest. But you may choose not to make this distinction in ladies over a certain age.

sisters living together:

The Misses Dean
Miss Davina Dean and Miss Daisy Dean
Again, if you are choosing the individual address, you should put the oldest first—but not if it risks the wrath of the sister concerned...

gentlemen:

Unfortunately, the etiquette for gentlemen reveals its age rather unflatteringly. The salutation for men remains as it has always has been, regardless of their single or married status. Sexist it may be, but at least it makes addressing envelopes easier.

Mr James Smith or James Smith, Esq., works for practically all men, unless he is:

Dr James Smith
Colonel James Smith
General James Smith
The Reverend (not Rev.) **James Smith**

children:

If children are invited, list their names under their parents' names on the invitation card. If your invitations do not have an inner envelope, list the children's names on the outer envelope.

informal invitations

The key to a good informal, or really personal, invitation is to include all the basic information your guests need—it can be easy to leave out crucial details in the enthusiasm of creativity. Ensure you include, at least:

• **The purpose of the invitation (ie, use the word "marriage," "wedding," "reception," or "party")**
• **The honorees (i.e., name bride and groom)**
• **The day and month, spelled out**
• **The time (and the time of the guests' departure, if necessary)**
• **The name and location of the venue**
• **Where to reply, and to whom, with contact details**
• **A reply-by date if you need one**

Classic invitations are printed—or, if you want to be very smart, engraved—in matt black on very thick card stock. But you can also have your invitations printed in any color, such as metallic silver, gold, pink, pewter, or bronze. If you choose a colored card, make sure the typeface color can be read against the background—metallics work well on black and dark papers.

guest contributions

If your invitees to the wedding are expected to contribute anything more than a gift—such as paying their share of a restaurant meal, bar tab, or hotel dinner—you should make this clear from the outset. Strictly speaking, they become co-hosts and the invitation wording should change to **"to share in a dinner to celebrate the marriage of"** or **"meet us in the** [name of venue] **for drinks."**

Include a priced version of the venue's menu, and check with the venue that the prices will be correct at the time of the wedding. And, for your own sake, attach an invitation response card to make bookings and reservations easier.

If your wedding is really informal, it can be fun to ask invitees to bring a dish for the buffet, or something to drink. Mark the invitation **"Potluck dinner."** To avoid remembering your wedding as the day you received 60 bowls of rice salad by 10am, coordinate dishes under headings such as **"entrée"** and **"dessert,"** although allow guests their creative freedom beyond that—don't be too specific.

replying to an invitation

The etiquette of acceptance has one abiding rule—the reply should always be in the manner of the invitation. Therefore, a formal request means a formal reply, while a truly informal invitation could include shrieks of delight at being invited, and a flood of fond feeling in a very personal style.

If you include a response card (see page 32), it should also reflect the style and wording of the invitation. If you are replying to an invitation formally (see pages 27–31), you should use a sheet of plain white paper.

FORMAL REPLY

Here is how to write a formal reply to a wedding invitation. You do not need to put anything else on the reply to the invitation, which should be on writing paper.

FORMAL REPLY WORDING
This is the set wording to either accept or decline a formal invitation.

....

thank

Mr and Mrs [husband's first name and surname of bride's parents]

for their kind invitation to the
marriage of their daughter
[first name of bride]

to Mr [groom's first name and surname]

at
[ceremony venue, not with address]
on
[day of week, month, day, time—do not include year]

and afterwards at
[name of reception venue, no address]

and have great pleasure in accepting/but regret they
are unable to attend

VARIATIONS ON REPLIES

Just as with the invitations, different wording is sometimes required for a reply according to the situation. These templates suggest ways to reply for each occasion. However you respond, make it prompt: the oldest tradition of all dictates that those who don't reply may risk an empty mailbox on the next occasion. It goes without saying that you should respond even if you are not going. When space may be scarce, particularly at a family wedding, it gives your host the opportunity to invite someone else.

LESS FORMAL REPLY
This can be used if the invitation was in a slightly less formal style.

[names of guests]
thank
Mr and Mrs [husband's first name and surname of bride's parents]
for their kind invitation to join them to celebrate
the marriage of their daughter

[first name of bride]
to Mr [groom's first name and surname]

[day of week], the [day] of [month]
at [time of day and ceremony venue with address]

and afterwards for a party at
[reception location and full address]

and have great delight in accepting

This is how to reply in an
informal manner.

[names of guests]
thank
Mr and Mrs [husband's first name and surname of bride's parents]
for their kind invitation to
the marriage of their daughter

on [day of week, month, day, time—do not include year]

and have great pleasure in accepting/
are delighted to accept/
regret a previous engagement means
they are unable to attend

[names of guests]
thank
Mrs [mother's first name and surname of bride] and
Mr [father's first name and surname of bride]
for their kind invitation to join them to celebrate
the marriage of their daughter
[first name of bride]
to Mr [groom's first name and surname]

[day of week], the [day] of [month]
at [time of day and ceremony venue with address]
and afterwards for a party at
[reception location and full address]

and have great delight in accepting

**REPLY TO DIVORCED
PARENTS**
How to respond when the
bride's parents are divorced.

[names of guests]
thank
Mr and Mrs [stepfather's first name and surname]
for their kind invitation to the marriage of her daughter
[bride's first name and surname]
to Mr [groom's first name and surname]

at [ceremony venue, not with address]
on [day of week, month, day, time—not year]

and afterwards at
[name of reception venue, no address]

and have great delight in accepting

REPLY TO A MOTHER AND STEPFATHER

This is the way to respond when the mother and stepfather are hosting the wedding.

REPLY TO THE BRIDE AND GROOM

Use this style when the invitation comes from the bride and groom themselves.

[names of guests]
thank
Miss [bride's first name and surname]
and
Mr [groom's first name and surname]
for their kind invitation to their marriage
on [day of week, month, day, time—not year]
at [ceremony venue, not with address]

and afterwards at
[name of reception location not full address]

and have great pleasure in accepting

REPLY TO A WEDDING RECEPTION INVITATION
Two replies are needed to respond to both the ceremony and the party.

[names of guests]
thank
Mr and Mrs [husband's first name and surname of bride's parents]
for their kind invitation to the
RESPONSE 1: the marriage of their daughter
RESPONSE 2: reception to celebrate the marriage of their daughter

[bride's first name]
to Mr [groom's first name and surname]

on [day of week] the [day] of [month]
at [time of day and name of reception location, not full address]

and have great pleasure in accepting

[names of guests]
thank
Mr and Mrs [husband's first name and surname of bride's parents]
for their kind invitation to the
reception to celebrate the marriage of
[first name of bride]
to
Mr [groom's first name and surname]

at [name of reception venue, no address]
on [day of week, month, day, and time—do not include year]

and have great pleasure in accepting

REPLY TO A POST-HONEYMOON RECEPTION
This is how to reply to an invitation to a reception that takes place some time after the wedding.

RESPONSE CARDS

To avoid making people write a reply to your
invitation, you could instead include a response
card for guests to send back to you.

RESPONSE CARD WORDING
Response cards can follow either of
these styles.

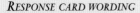

will be
able/unable
to accept your kind wedding invitation

Please respond by
[month/day]

Thank you so much
for your kind wedding invitation
We will/will not be
able to attend

Please respond by
[month/day]

additions

In times gone by, smart invitations did not include much in the way of practical detail—the address of the church was seen to be unnecessary as everyone went every week, or it was in the family's garden. The smartest weddings were held in the family's historic chapel, usually to be found on the ground floor next to the room dedicated equally fervently to rubber boots. And everybody knew where the reception was—if it were held at home, the dwelling concerned would probably be visible from 50 miles away, so no problem there. Hotel receptions, which are a relatively new invention for the upper classes (appearing around 1900), posed no worries either—all Londoners knew where the Ritz was, for instance—and if you didn't, you probably weren't quite the sort of person one would ask to one's wedding.

Nowadays, it is perfectly normal to enclose a flyer with more details about the wedding. You might choose to include:

• Wedding list at a store of your choosing
• A map showing the ceremony venue, with marked route to the reception
• List of local taxi firms plus route from nearest city, airport, or bus or train station
• A range of accommodation, from the humblest motel room to the grandest hotel
• Parking details

including a menu

If your caterers are small, or indeed are your own family, including a menu with choices from the wedding meal can be useful. Ideally, be as descriptive as possible about the dishes, or use the caterers' exact names for each course to give guests the best idea of what they would enjoy most. You may also want to include allergy information, and to specify which options are suitable for vegetarians. Guests can make their choices and return the menu with their response cards.

services of blessing

If you choose to have the marriage blessed, invitations follow this wording.

Mr and Mrs [husband's first name and surname of bride's parents]
request the pleasure of your company at
a service of blessing following the marriage of
[first name of bride]
to
Mr [groom's first name and surname]

at [name of ceremony venue, no address]
on [day of week, month, day, time—do not include year]

RSVP
[include phone number/email address]

marriage announcement

If you have large numbers of family abroad, or are holding a small wedding, you can mark the day with a newspaper announcement. As with an engagement, this is a fast, inexpensive, and efficient way to broadcast your good news. Usually, publications will issue you with an online form to complete, but you can also use this formal wording:

Mr [initials and last name of groom] and Miss [initials and last name of bride]
The Marriage was held on [day of week, month, day, and year] at [name of ceremony venue, town, and country] between [first name of groom] son of Mr and Mrs [first name and surname of groom's father] of [town and country] and [first name of bride] daughter of Mr and Mrs [first name and surname of bride's father] of [town and country].

wedding favor tags: the wording

Favor tags should reflect your invitations, the spirit of the day, and your personalities.

You may wish to simply include the bride and groom's first names and the date, or you could add **"Thank you for being with us today"** before the names. Some people choose to also include a favorite line or two from a poem, a religious verse, or an extract from the ceremony reading.

making favor tags

You will need:
• **Card stock to match your wedding invitations and color scheme**
• **A reel of thin matching ribbon**
• **Craft glue**
• **Holepuncher**
• **Scissors**

You will also need a PC and color printer.

1) Using your computer's word processing program, experiment with the layout for your wording, using fonts and typeface sizes that match the invitation. You should be able to fit several tags into one sheet of card.
2) Once you have created one that works well with the size of the tag, print copies of the design, cut them out, and affix them to the card stock.
3) Punch a hole in the top of each tag.
4) Cut the card into individual tags.
5) Tie your tag to each favor with the ribbon.

Tip: Use this technique to create place cards, maps, or direction sheets, programs, pamphlets, and thank-you cards.

A CHRISTENING
announcing the new arrival

Unlike wedding invitations, which are a minefield of etiquette for the unwary, christening and naming invitations follow a more relaxed style. Nowadays, many people prefer to send out birth announcements to all, while christenings are, as ever, for the select few. This section illustrates the choices you have.

birth announcement card

Ideal for illustration, these announcements can be immeasurably improved with a photograph of the baby, a family group, or a tiny footprint. Whatever you choose to decorate your new arrival's entry into the world, be sure to include: the baby's first name and surname; the sex of the baby (if the name doesn't make this clear); his or her weight in pounds and ounces—include kilos if you think anyone will understand them; the date and time of birth; the parents' full names.

You could also include a quote from a spiritual source or a favorite poem (such as on page 41).

did you know?

Even true dictators of etiquette concede that christening invitations take a less formal form, since traditionally christenings were held in the local place of worship on Saturdays or Sundays as part of the service, and any respectable person was meant to be already firmly seated. The idea that one would need directions would, in fact, be seen as an appalling slur on one's morals, as would the idea that a guest—as a close friend or family member—would need the address of the party, always held in the mother or grandmother's home.

birth announcements

With many couples having friends and family spread far and wide, a newspaper announcement can save time for an exhausted new mother. The formal wording contains the mother's maiden name, if she is married, which helps readers identify the family.

The correct form is:

[SURNAME OF BABY] On [day of week, month, day, year] to [first name of mother] née [mother's maiden name] and [first name of father] a daughter/son [all first names of baby], a sister/brother for [first name only of siblings].

If the parents are unmarried, use this form instead:

[SURNAME OF BABY] On [day of week, month, day, year] to [first and last name of mother] and [first and last name of father] a daughter/son [all first names of baby or all first names and surname of baby], a sister/brother for [first name only of siblings].

INVITATIONS TO A CHRISTENING

If you do want to send out invitations to a christening, use one of the versions given here as required, which are not too formal but which still provide all the necessary information.

CLASSIC CHRISTENING INVITATION
This is the form for a christening in church, followed by a gathering at the parents' home.

[name of guests in handwriting]

Mr and Mrs [husband's first name and surname]

request the pleasure of your company
at the christening of their son/daughter
[first name of baby]

at
[place of worship, not with address]

on
[day of week, month, day, time—do not include year]

and afterwards at home
[time]

RSVP
[parents' address]
[include phone number/email address]

"Every good and perfect gift is from above."

[name of guests in handwriting]

Ms/Mrs [mother's first name and surname]
and Mr [husband's first name and surname]
request the pleasure of your company
at the christening of their son/daughter
[first and last name of baby]

at [place of worship, not with address]
on [day of week, month, day, time—do not include year]

and afterwards at home
[time]

RSVP
[parents' address]
[include phone number/email address]

Mr and Mrs [husband's first name and surname]
request the pleasure of the company of
[name of guests]

at the christening of their son/daughter
[first name of baby]

at [place of worship and address]
on [day of week, month, day, time—do not include year]

and afterwards at home
[time]

RSVP
[include phone number/email address]

A BAT OR BAR MITZVAH
the perfect etiquette

Known as the coming-of-age ceremony for children, Bar Mitzvah and Bat Mitzvah celebrations mark the day when, officially now adults, the "Bar" (son) and "Bat" (daughter) are ready to observe the commandments—"Mitzvah"—of the Jewish faith. Taking place at the age of 12 for girls and 13 for boys, an elaborate ceremony followed by a party or reception is fairly modern, certainly by the standards of Jewish history, only becoming popular in the 20th century. This section explains how to invite people to this important event.

how to invite people

The order of your invitations should run following the list given here:
• **An opening verse, to include the Bar or Bat Mitzvah's name**
• **Synagogue address, or other place of worship**
• **The name and address of the reception venue**
• **The date and time of the service**
• **Whether you are including a kiddush**
• **The time of the reception**
• **"Please reply by [date]"with your name and address**

In Orthodox and Hasidic circles, women are not allowed to attend a Bar Mitzvah; if you are a guest unsure of the community's customs, check with the local rabbi. Gifts are, however, a pretty universal custom, given at the reception. If you want to give money, a nice touch is to offer it in multiples of 18, an auspicious number in Judaism. The Bat or Bar Mitzvah takes place within the Sabbath service, so many of the people present may not be involved in the Bar Mitzvah and do not need invitations to the reception.

verses for the bar or bat mitzvah invitation

Choose from these sample verses to begin your invitation:

Please join us in
worship as our
son/daughter
[insert first name]
is called to the
Torah as a
Bar/Bat Mitzvah

[insert parents' name]
request that you join us
in worship as our
son/daughter
[insert first name]
is called to the
Torah as a
Bar/Bat Mitzvah

We invite you to share
our happiness as our
son/daughter
[insert first name]
is called to the
Torah as a
Bar/Bat Mitzvah

You can also send invitations from the boy or girl:

My family and I would like you to share our pride and joy
on the occasion of my Bar/Bat Mitzvah

a jewish baby naming

Jewish naming invitations begin with traditional verses, or religious extracts. You should then include:

1. The full name of both parents
2. The baby's name, with (optional) Hebrew name
3. The name and address of the house of worship
4. The address of the reception
5. The date and time of the ceremony and the reception
6. RSVP details

Here are some sample verses that could begin the invitation.

From generation to generation
We carry on
With the richness of tradition
And the promise of tomorrow
Please join us
as our son/daughter
[Baby's name]
is given his/her [Hebrew] name

We invite you to share
this special day
as our son/daughter
[Baby's name]
is given his/her [Hebrew] name

With pride and joy,
we invite you to
share our happiness
as our son/daughter
[Baby's name]
is given his/her [Hebrew] name

A WEDDING ANNIVERSARY
looking back over the years

Wedding anniversaries are a one-time only, unmissable opportunity to have a great party. And the key to a good anniversary party is to send the invitations out as early as possible. This is the chance for you and your spouse to look back over the years and forward to pastures new with a unique gathering of all your old friends, family, and descendants, so giving people plenty of notice about the party will ensure a good turnout.

planning ahead

With this kind of celebration, the guest list is vital, because couples want to celebrate years of happiness with all their nearest and dearest. For this reason, the "Save the Date" card comes into its own—after all, you know in advance when the special day will be, and, in order to secure everyone's attendance, can fix a party date and send cards out up to six months, or even a year, in advance. Invitations sent out three months in advance are not unusual.

Remember to use an invitation form that gives the year of the occasion in all your correspondence and to send it far in advance. If you are an adult child following the tradition of hosting a silver or golden anniversary party for your parents, see page 49 for the wording of the invitation.

It is particularly important to specify a preference for receiving gifts on an anniversary invitation. Couples who have shared a house for years may not want piles of knick-knacks that just add to dusting duties, and the trend for downsizing means many people are actively trying to streamline their possessions. However, since suggesting that you might be expecting a present is the height of bad manners in any circumstances except a wedding, you may want to state **"No gifts please."**

save the date card

Depending on how formal you want to be, choose from one of these wordings:

SAVE THE DATE

Betty
and Bill Bird
have been married for
(25/40/50/60) years
September 23, 2016 is our
(Silver/Ruby/Golden/Diamond)
Anniversary

Invitation to follow

SAVE THE DATE

We are delighted to
announce
that we will be
celebrating
(25/40/50/60) years
of marriage
September 23, 2016

Invitation to follow
Betty and Bill Bird

SAVE THE DATE

September 23, 2016
Betty and Bill Bird
(Silver/Ruby/Golden/Diamond) Anniversary
Invitation to follow

SAVE THE DATE

September 23, 2016
is our
(Silver/Ruby/
Golden/Diamond)
Anniversary
and we would like you to
join us
Betty and Bill

Invitation to follow

cotton, copper, or diamonds?

Wedding anniversaries and what they mean

In times gone by, particularly special wedding anniversaries were marked by gifts that marked the number of years the couple had been married. The husband would present his wife with a treat, which grew in value as the marriage grew in length. Nowadays, most relatively new wives would be pretty horrified by a reel of cotton, indeed possibly to the point that a diamond wedding would begin to look unlikely, but silver, gold, ruby, and diamond celebrations are still celebrated with their traditional symbols. Use the list below to inspire the coloring and illustration of your invitations:

First anniversary——Paper
Second——Cotton
Third——Leather
Fourth——Linen
Fifth——Wood
Sixth——Iron
Seventh——Wool or copper
Eighth——Bronze
Ninth——Pottery
Tenth——Tin

Past the ten-year mark….
Eleventh——Steel
Twelfth——Silk
Thirteenth——Lace
Fourteenth——Ivory
Fifteenth——Crystal
Twentieth——China
25th——Silver
30th——Pearls
35th——Coral
40th——Ruby
45th——Sapphire
50th——Gold
60th——Diamond [in UK]

And for those with true endurance…
70th——Platinum
75th——Diamond [in US]
80th——Oak

If you are attending an anniversary party as a guest, use the symbol or number of years to inspire a fitting present. Think laterally—a silver wedding anniversary, for instance, can be celebrated with 25 weeks' of movie tickets, while a pair of golden rose bushes, blooming each year in the month of their marriage, will remind a happy couple of 50 years' worth of continuing marital triumph.

Anniversary Invitations

This section provides ways to invite guests to your anniversary celebrations.

FORMAL VERSION
Classic wording for a party held at the couple's home.

Mr and Mrs [husband's first name and surname]

request the pleasure of your company
at the celebrations of their
[Silver / Ruby / Golden / Diamond] *Anniversary*
on
[day of week, month, day, and year]
at home
[time]

RSVP

[include phone number / email address]

No gifts please

[as required]

Mr and Mrs *[husband's first name and surname]*
request the pleasure of the company of

[names of guests]

at the celebration of their
[Silver/Ruby/Golden/Diamond] Anniversary
on *[day of week, month, day, and year]*

at home
[time]

RSVP
[include phone number/email address]
No gifts please *[as required]*

INFORMAL VERSION
Many people prefer to use this friendlier version.

REAFFIRMATION SERVICE INVITATION
If you are including a reaffirmation service as part of the celebrations, use this form.

Mr and Mrs *[husband's first name and surname]*
request the pleasure of the company of
[names of guests]
at a service of reaffirmation of their marriage
at *[name of ceremony venue, no address]*
on *[day of week, month, day, and year]*

and afterwards at a reception
[name of venue]
for their
[Silver/Ruby/Golden/Diamond] Anniversary

RSVP
[include phone number/email address]
No gifts please *[as required]*

Replying to the Invitation

As with any invitation, the reply should be in the manner of the invitation; a formal invitation means a formal reply, and so on. However, even a very informal invitation requires a timely, clear reply.

FORMAL REPLY
Hosts can also use this formal reply as a response card if necessary.

[names of guests]
thank
Mr and Mrs [husband's first name and surname]

for their kind invitation to the
[Silver / Ruby / Golden / Diamond] *Anniversary*
on
[day of week, month, day, and year]
at home / at
[reception venue, not with address]
on [day of week, month, day, time—do not include year]

and have great pleasure in accepting /
but regret they are unable to attend

[names of guests]

thank
Mr and Mrs [husband's first name and surname]
for their kind invitation to the
[Silver / Ruby / Golden / Diamond]
anniversary

at [time of day and ceremony venue with address]

and have great delight in accepting

INFORMAL REPLY
For a slightly more informal approach, use this form.

RESPONSE CARDS
These can be short and to the point.

. . . .

will be
able / unable
to accept your kind
anniversary invitation

Please respond by
[month / day]

. . . .

Thank you so much
for your kind invitation

We will / will not be
able to attend

A BIRTHDAY PARTY
another year wiser

Unlike other momentous occasions, birthday parties are not ruled with the same iron rod of etiquette as much as, say, a wedding. While you can produce a formal "at home" invitation (see page 56), it is often more fun to make free with convention and produce an entirely unique, one-off invitation. This section shows you how to create a truly successful birthday party invitation for a birthday girl or boy of any age—and gives you several ideas on how you can make someone feel extra-special before the party has even started.

party essentials

If there's one constant in human nature, it's wanting to be made a fuss of on your birthday. This longing does not apply just to children— far from it—everyone wants to be made to feel important, pampered, and a little spoiled. Requirements include a cake, an interestingly shaped gift (if not several), and, most of all, a party. Unlike other social occasions, which tend to be family- or couple-centered, the birthday party is usually a celebration of someone in their own right as an individual, and so the birthday party invitation can reflect this.

However, before you do anything clever to your invitation, include the following vital information: the names of the host(s); the point of the party— that is, the birthday, possibly with the honoree's age (after the age of 9, it is not necessary to include an age, except for 18th and 21st birthday parties); the day, and date and time, spelled out; and finally, the address or name of the venue.

hosting a party for others

The wording for holding a celebration for others runs in this order:

1. The name of the host(s)
2. The nature of the celebrations, i.e., birthday, anniversary, or reunion
3. The name of the honorees, those for whom the party is being thrown (if different)
4. The date and time spelled out to avoid confusion (include the year if the party is more than three months away)
5. The name of the venue

Tip: If you are hosting a party for a lady, it may be considered rude to mention her age after she has passed the age of 45. Always ask first.

how to get a person into an envelope

Celebrating a birthday is really paying tribute to one person's uniqueness and finer qualities. Your invitation should reflect this; try these ideas to bring out the person behind the party.

First impressions count. You want as many acceptances as possible, so create an invitation with impact. Use photographs of the birthday girl or boy as a montage to create a splash with a series of snaps showing them through the years.

You can also experiment with color and design, but don't sacrifice the key details to prettiness—your goal is to get guests to arrive.

Another way to create a memorable invitation is not to stick to the classic card shape. For instance, if the honoree is a literary type, make your invitation into an historic scroll with a ribbon tie, or cut handbag-shaped cards for a city girl. Alternatively, fold invitations as simple

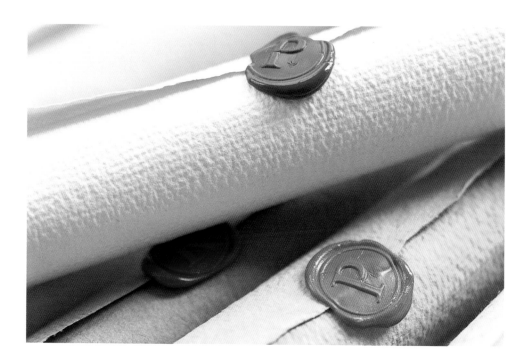

origami shapes that reflect the birthday girl or boy's keenest interests: a sailor's invitation can be folded into a boat, or a cook's into a chef's hat. Invitations in the shape of the honoree's first name initial are individual and work for everyone.

Rather than a card, you could instead mail guests a "mystery" object that sums up the guest of honor as the invitation, attaching a tag with the party details. Used by PR agencies as a publicity tactic for their clients' luxury goods, this will always get your invitation the attention it deserves. The secret lies in not agonizing about choosing a "wacky" object—opening mail that doesn't contain paper will be quirky enough for your guests. For example, a gardener could be represented with a single silk bloom or a package of flower seeds; a fisherman with a bright feather fly; a runner with a neat twist of shoelaces. Bear in mind when shopping for your "mysteries" that they should weigh little, be inexpensive and unbreakable by mail, and that the tag can be attached firmly. Or, why not send edible invitations? Bake a batch of large, plain cookies and ice them with the invitation details, then deliver them in small bakers' boxes. If you don't cook, use candy wrapped in tissue. For children with health-conscious parents, send a piece of fruit with paper "leaves" that contain the details. As with the mystery object invitations, attach a tag with the details repeated—greedy guests may fail to show up otherwise.

To focus on the birthday girl or boy, send a silhouette of the honoree as the invitation. Elegant and easy to make, you can give a copy as a birthday present, which will also provide a permanent reminder of the party. You will need a photograph of the honoree in profile, sheets of black and cream card, a black marker, paper glue, and a craft knife. Photocopy the photograph, then shade in the profile in black, making sure you have a clean, defined line on all sides. Scalpel out your silhouette, and photocopy it once per invitation. Cut out the profiles and glue them onto ovals of cream card. Fold the black card in two, and stick each oval on the front, then use metallic inks to write the party details inside the card. Another idea is to create a fake "magazine cover" starring the honoree as the cover star. The issue edition can be the party date, the main headline the party announcement, and the straplines vehicles for jokes or quotations. Include the time, location, and RSVP essentials on the back.

FORMAL BIRTHDAY INVITATION

You may choose to send a formal, "at home" invitation.

FORMAL INVITATION WORDING
Use this for a formal birthday celebration.

did you know?

RSVP is a French abbreviation for the phrase: "Répondez s'il vous plaît"—that is, "Please reply."

Miss Polly Parker
requests the pleasure of your company
at the celebration of her [30th] birthday
on [day of week, month, and day]
at home
[time]

RSVP
[include phone number/email address]

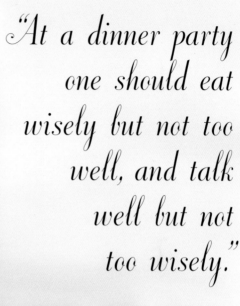

"At a dinner party one should eat wisely but not too well, and talk well but not too wisely."

WILLIAM SOMERSET MAUGHAM
(1874–1965)

a children's birthday party

Many children's parties are themed, and choosing the invitation marks your choice. So before you make your final choice, make sure you can coordinate your theme with these other party items:

- Outdoor or yard decoration as well as indoor room decoration
- Party bags that can be given out to all the guests at the end of the party
- Various games, each with prizes
- Napkins, tablecloth, and paper plates, cups, bowls, and platters
- Food and drink, within reason: a party may not be the best time to introduce a small child to a particularly exotic world cuisine. Stick to familiar favorites if in doubt.

- The cake: Remember to make use of the theme throughout, not just on the frosting. For example, a princess cake for a small girl will inspire shrieks of delight if, thanks to four or five drops of food coloring, the sponge insides are bright pink too; while a spaceship cake can conceal a hollowed out "power source" with marshmallow "fuel pods" and a jelly drop "control panel." For safety's sake, include only edible extras inside the cake. You are aiming for gasps of delight, not a choking child.

a surprise party

Of all the most delightful parties, and truly unforgettable, is the surprise birthday party. The key to a successful invitation is keeping the secret while maximizing the anticipation; so follow these wordings and invitation styles to avoid letting the cat out of the bag.

the seven golden rules of surprise party invitations

1. Begin the invitation with "Top Secret," "Sshhhh...," or "Urgent and Confidential"—all phrases which will stress the secrecy, but not dim the excitement.
2. Give a cell phone number and a date by which guests should reply. Ruthlessly chase tardy respondents well before the party so that, not only will you get the firm numbers you need to plan for in secret, the honoree will not be alerted by a stream of suspicious calls from old friends on the day of the party. You could also set up a dedicated email address for replies. Marking the invitation "Acceptances only" may be helpful, too.
3. Include the start time of the party and the time of arrival of the guest of honor, so that all the guests will know they have to be gathered well in advance.
4. Include local parking spots in the invitation, so that guests can park far from the venue in order to avoid raising the honoree's suspicions.
5. If the party is themed, mention it prominently, so that guests can offer contributions or prepare their costumes well in advance of the occasion.
6. Warn guests if they will have to contribute financially or share the costs of the meal—there are some surprises no one needs, and if you are keeping the party details to yourself, invitees may assume you are sponsoring the whole occasion. Include menu details (with sample costs) if you are holding a restaurant dinner.
7. Make sure all bookings with restaurants or caterers are confirmed before you draft the invitation. Then use the template below and ask a friend to check it—nothing is more guaranteed to let slip the secret than having to contact all the guests repeatedly.

SURPRISE PARTY INVITATION

You don't have to use the wording of a formal invitation, so indulge your creativity, but always make sure the essential details are included.

Top secret/Sshhhh.../Urgent and confidential
[first name and surname of host(s) and hostess(es)]
invite [name of guest] to the Surprise Party for [name of honoree]
[occasion—for example, 40th birthday]
on [day of week, month, day, and year] at [location, plus address] at [time]
(Honoree will be arriving at [time], so please be prompt.)

RSVP by [date] to [hosts'/hostesses' first name]
[include cell number/dedicated email address] [theme/parking details—as required]
No gifts please/Acceptances only [add as required]
[include dinner menu with pricing/contribution costs—as required]

A REUNION
bringing together old friends

Heralding an event that begins with anticipation and ends with memories that last for life, your reunion invitations should get the attention they deserve. Once you have picked the time and place, mail the invitations as soon as possible. Like anniversaries, the secret to a good reunion is the collection of guests, and your invitees deserve the chance to juggle their schedules, and to plan their vacations and travel arrangements ahead of time. You can also use a "Save the Date" card (see page 47) to maximize the chances of a good turnout.

reunion essentials

As ever, before you start theming or decorating your invitation, include the essentials:

- The names of the host(s) and hostess(es)
- The purpose of the reunion—family, class, friends, neighbors, social or hobby groups, military or professional reunions.
- The day of the week, and day and time, spelled to avoid confusion, e.g., Saturday–Sunday, May first to third, 2012
- The address or name of the venue, plus a map
- Your contact details, in full, with name, address, telephone, and email address

Further details of what the reunion will entail can also be included in your invitation. As many reunions nowadays last for a weekend, and are packed with scheduled fun for different age groups as well as a central dinner, your guests will appreciate the chance to be fully prepared.

You could provide your guests with a list of planned events (always state these are optional: many among us find group games, or sports, shamefully difficult), which will allow guests to bring—or purchase in advance—whatever clothes or sports equipment that may be needed.

Include a note if there is a smart party for which men could wear suits and ladies evening dresses, as well as practical items such as warm sweaters, thick socks, or swimwear. If you are expecting small children, remind parents to bring a high chair, cot, bedding, and infant food if these are not provided.

As some guests are bound to be traveling long distances, take the opportunity to include transportation details and local train/bus/plane details—many people appreciate the chance to book a cheaper fare. Include a list of nearby taxi firms, too. It can also be helpful to tell guests the likely costs of meals and activities (if any), allowing them to budget accordingly.

If you are holding a family reunion, ask each relation to collect their old photographs and any portable heirlooms for display. Remind them to nametag each of their precious portraits and knick-knacks.

Finally, ensure that you include a thank-you note in advance to your guests for their attendance. Ask a colleague or friend to proofread the invitations before you print and mail them.

REUNION INVITATION

Follow the templates provided to word invitations and response cards for a reunion. Ensure that you include the year, since these invitations should be sent long before the event.

REUNION INVITATION WORDING
Follow the style below for your reunion invitations.

RESPONSE CARDS
You can also supply reply cards with informal wording that is brief and to the point.

. . . .

*will be
able/unable
to accept your kind
reunion invitation*

*Please respond by
[month/day]*

[first name and surname of host(s) and hostess(es)]
[name of the committee/organization, if required]
invite
[name of guest(s)]
to the Reunion for
[name of family/clan/class/charity, or other occasion
if there is one, such as a school's 50th anniversary]
on [day of week/weekend, month, day, and year]
at [location, plus address]
[time]

RSVP *by* [date] *to* [hosts'/hostessess' first nsme]
[include address, phone number/email address]
[cost per guest/family, if applicable]
Acceptances only [as required]

create a reunion reminder

In addition to the invitation, a reminder card can be very useful. A few weeks before the reunion, send a card or email in the same style, repeating the time and date. Make sure your guests are fully prepared by including the following: the full invitation details repeated; a note of the predicted weather forecast, with a rough guide of the temperature; a timetable of all the events; a map of the area. If anyone complains about being reminded (inevitably the most chaotic guest), smoothly explain that you are sending the reminders to everyone and that it isn't personal.

reunion: welcome hints

While sending a tingle of excitement down the spine, reunions can be a little intimidating for more timid guests. Follow these tips to put everyone at ease—and note that you should theme nametags, quizzes, and guest directories in the same way as your invitation to provide an elegant occasion, as well as enduring reminders of the reunion.

If you can, organize some guests as "greeters" to make sure everyone feels really welcome, and hand out disposable cameras to all—including children over the age of seven—and remind everyone to snap away. You may wish to nametag guests. While most people secretly find it helpful, many could see it as a little officious. Get around this with humor: include the guest's photo from a distant wedding/their senior yearbook/their teenage years, so they can be recognized without feeling like a store clerk.

Set aside a display area where you can show off all the portraits, photos, memorabilia, yearbook photos, and so on that you have collected and your guests have brought with them. If one of the guests is too sick or busy to attend, make them a card in the style of the invitation, address it, and leave it open by the display area for other guests to sign. Mail it to the absentee after the event.

Many people will want to keep in touch after the event. A good way to do this and provide a reminder of the reunion is to create a directory of the guest list, including everyone's contact details, which guests can collect as they leave. You could theme the guest directory in the style of the invitation.

boost your guest list: the cornell university technique

Some years ago, The Cornell University Class of 1998 Committee sent their past schoolmates this reunion invitation.

"Want to come to Reunion on the house? We are looking for the classmate who can provide current contact information for the greatest number of our classmates. The winner will receive complimentary reunion registration for one (meals, registration fee, University fee, etc., not including accommodation)."

Designed to boost numbers, the "contest invitation" ended with a reply deadline date and return address to which all the lists of new contacts were sent. Figures are not known, but anecdotal evidence suggests the technique has been widely used since.

SCHOOL'S OUT
celebrating achievements

The end of education is a time to celebrate all that you've achieved with your friends and family. The prom is often one of the most memorable moments in school life, and so it is important that all goes according to plan—which begins with the invitations. Similarly, graduation, both from school and college, is the culmination of years of hard work, and it is only natural to invite your nearest and dearest to share in your pride and happiness.

the prom

Among the most long-standing of traditions at high schools, the prom has its own heritage of etiquette. And many students will keep their prom invitation as a keepsake that symbolizes their high school years. Both boys and girls can ask each other, and whoever does—the host—will pay for the dinner, prom tickets, and corsages. If you are a teacher or member of staff distributing invitations, mail them at least a month before the big night.

While there are many styles and wording, the most elegant is generally agreed to be classic, semi-formal wording, with the only addition being the mention of the celebration's theme.

Anything goes for decoration purposes—and, once you have finalized the wording you may wish to hold a class competition to see who can create the most stylish invitation around it.

add to your invitation

Once you have your invitation, assemble a mini Prom Kit for your best friends, or present this to your partner, to accompany it. Include a camera (with a USB cord), a money clip, and a keepsake brag book, then add the photos and the gossip in the brag book to your invitations as a memento.

PROM INVITATION

If you wish, you can stick to straightforward wording: "The graduating class of [school] invites you to the Senior Prom of 2010, to be held on [date] at [location]." However, for a little more style, use one of the templates given here.

The Junior/Senior Class
[name of school]
requests the pleasure of your company/
requests the honor of your presence
at the Junior/Senior Prom
on [day of week and date, spelled out]
[year]
at
([time]o'clock in the evening)
[address]
["theme"]

The Senior Class
[name of school]
cordially invites you to
["theme"]

Junior-Senior Prom
on [day of week and date, spelled out]
[year]
at
([time]o'clock in the evening)
[address]

"It takes courage to grow up and become who you really are."

e.e. cummings (1894–1962)

a graduation invitation

One of life's great achievements, a graduation should be celebrated in style. Your invitation should, while not being over-serious, reflect the formality of the ceremony and be suitable as a keepsake to make the day memorable.

The invitations will be either to the ceremony, followed by a tea party or drinks outdoors, or simply to the party.

GRADUATION INVITATIONS

Invitations generally take three forms: the first and most common is from parents or carers if they are the hosts; the second is used when the graduate is holding the party themselves; while the third is reserved for invitations sent out by the school, which students can pass on. If you send invitations to your own graduation or school departure, a little less formality is in order. You can add a touch of humor by including a funny quotation, or take the opportunity to thank your family for their support in print.

FROM THE PARENTS
This is the most common form of invitation to a graduation.

Mr and Mrs [father's first name and surname, or mother's first name and surname and father's first name and surname (if divorced)]

invite

[name of guest(s)]

to the

graduation of their [daughter/son]

on [day of week, month, day, and year]

at [time]

at

[school's address/auditorium address]

and afterwards for a party

at

[home address or venue with address]

RSVP by
[date]
[include parents' address, phone number/email address]

FROM THE GRADUATE

This can be made a little less formal with an amusing quotation or with a thank you to the graduate's family.

FROM THE CLASS

These invitations are sent out by the school.

[first and surname of graduate]
requests the pleasure of your company/
requests the honor of your presence
at
his/her graduation
[name of guest(s)]
on [day of week, month, day, and year]
at [time]
at
[school's address/auditorium address]

and afterwards for a party
at
[your chosen venue with address]

RSVP by
[date]
[graduate's phone number/email address]

The Senior Class of [year]
[name of school] High School
invite you to attend
Graduation/Commencement Exercises
on [day of week, month, day, and year]
at [time]
at
[school's address/auditorium address]

and afterwards for a party
at
[the committee's chosen venue with address]

RSVP by
[date]
[committee's email address]

RESPONSE CARDS

Reply cards take a simple, straightforward form.

....

will be
able/unable
to accept your kind
graduation invitation

Please respond by
[month/day]

A HOUSEWARMING
settling into your new home

No less momentous than a wedding in these days of high mortgages—and in many cases, too, the nearest many modern couples will get to one—the housewarming combines the best of a formal occasion—the celebration of a life achievement successfully negotiated—with all the laid-back fun of a night on the couch.

ways to a beautiful home (in an envelope, at least)

Remember that although no one expects your new home to be beautifully decorated, particularly if you are surrounded by boxes, your invitation can still be perfectly stylish; just follow the decoration tips given here.

If you're artistic, illustrate the invitation with a drawing of the front door or a sketch of you and your family standing outside your new home. Or, using your favorite interior magazine and a color photocopier, mock up a magazine cover with a stylish living room as the cover shot. Give the party date as the edition (top left), the party announcement as the main headline, and paste the map, the time, location,

and RSVP essentials on the back. This works best if your home is in "pre-decoration stage"— indeed, the worse the condition of your home, the more amused the guests tend to be.

A nice idea, if you have managed any refurbishment, or even a touch of gardening, is to send out a folded card with a "before" photograph on the front, and the "after" on the main page. If, instead, you are still mid-renovation, save spare paint and sample pots, and, using a ⅛-inch (1-cm) brush, "paint" your invitation wording onto squares of wallpaper remnants. Allow them to dry for 36 hours before you mail them.

HOUSEWARMING INVITATION WORDING

Your invitation needs one practical essential for the festivities to go smoothly: a map, as many invitees will not have been to your new home. Otherwise, the invitation goes as a standard informal party invitation, although you may wish to add a touch of individuality with a funny quotation of some sort.

[first name and surname (optional) of host(s) and hostess(es)]

invite

[name of guest(s)]

to their housewarming

on [day of week, month, day]

at [address]

[time]

RSVP *by* [date] *to* [hosts'/hostessess' first nsme]

[telephone, cell number/dedicated email address]

[include map]

HOUSEWARMING INVITATION
Use this classic party invitation wording and personalize it with your own decoration.

CHAPTER 2

Letters for Life

Faced with one of life's challenges, be it at work or home, we all struggle to find the right words; indeed, the nuances of etiquette over the ages can be easy to master compared to finding a true, personal voice. While the secret to much correspondence—invitations, professional communications, and so on—is about getting it right in a formal or traditional way, the key to other types of letters is usually authenticity. This chapter shows you how to express yourself so that your recipient feels truly valued.

Get-well Letters
offering words of comfort

Get-well letters, or letters to those facing surgery or recovering from an illness, can be difficult to write, but will always be a joy to receive. Isn't the best therapy of all affection and caring? If you are hesitant about putting pen to paper, remember that your letter is a little piece of healing in its own right. Your written expressions of love and concern, tidbits of news or gossip from outside the hospital or sickroom, and your enduring love and best wishes, cannot fail to boost the spirits of the patient. Use these tips to help you create a letter that will inspire a friend, family member, colleague, or loved one to recovery all the sooner.

a letter for hope and healing

Start by detailing your regret that the person has been injured or fallen sick; if it was sudden, do mention this. No matter how formal your relationship is with the sick person, your letter can and should show affection. You can do this by explaining briefly how concerned you are, and letting the person know you are thinking of them. Be respectful of the patient's vulnerable state. Don't dwell on the illness, or your worry, if it is serious; keep the tone positive, bright, and focused on recovery.

Mention the latest news about the parts of your life you share; if you are writing to family or a friend, give them a "newsletter" update of what mutual friends have been up to. Stick to the fun parts of recent activities, and point out what they would have liked most had they been there. You could also tell the person how much they are

missed; reiterate that you are looking forward to seeing them up and running soon. Mention upcoming events that you hope they might be able to make, but tell them you will provide a full report in case they are still not up to it.

If you wish, take a few lines to express your heartfelt appreciation to the patient for how much they mean to you; point out, for instance, how loyal, funny, and kind they are as a friend, or how great they are to work with, or how much their return is anticipated at family gatherings.

To keep your letter cheerful, include light-hearted diversions you think the patient might enjoy. Recount a funny story you saw in the paper (and include the clipping), tell the latest office joke, or even summarize recent episodes of their all-time favorite TV show. Also, suggest easy and

effort-free cheer for their convalescence: offer them a good book or DVD that you think they might enjoy for their convalescence, and perhaps mention new websites or music, too.

If you feel that you can't produce anything amusing—reasonable enough under the circumstances—you could include an inspiring quote, such as: "Enjoy convalescence. It is the part that makes the illness worthwhile." (George Bernard Shaw, 1856–1950)

As you bring your letter to a close, you may also want to repeat that the person is in your thoughts and, if necessary, prayers. Mention mutual friends and acquaintances and pass on their best wishes, too. Finish by offering practical help, if appropriate, and wishing the person a very speedy and comfortable recovery.

GET-WELL LETTER:

Having read the advice on pages 72–3, you should have in mind your own thoughts and reflections, and an idea of what you and your reader are both interested in. Now use the template given here to frame a handwritten letter that supports your own expressions and feelings.

GET-WELL LETTER TEMPLATE
This template provides a structure and wording that you can personalize.

[your address]

[date]

Dear _____,

I am so sorry to hear that you were sick/in the hospital/learn of your accident. I do hope you are feeling better now that your treatment has started and you are in the good hands of the doctors.

Everyone at school/work/in the family joins me in sending our very best love/wishes to you at this difficult time and I/we hope you are not feeling too bad.

I saw our friends/family/workmates recently and we all went out to the [example: local Italian restaurant]. You would have enjoyed it. [explain why; for instance: "The owner burst into song when he heard it was Marlene's birthday..."]

We all missed you—you are such a great friend/colleague. [explain why] Your thoughtfulness/generosity/kindness touches so many people's lives, and everyone is always so pleased to see you.

I hope your convalescence is going well. Have you seen/read [DVD/book]? If not, I could lend it to you. Are you up to date with [favorite TV show]? [add, for example: "Tell me if you need your fix of 'Gossip Girl' and I'll update you."]

Let me know if you need anything—or if I can bring anything to your bedside to make the days more interesting.

As ever, everyone at school/home/work sends you their very best, as I do, for a fast recovery. You are in all our thoughts and prayers.

Love/With best wishes/Sincerely,

[signature]

LETTERS OF CONDOLENCE
finding the right words

Sending your condolences in writing creates an extremely important, landmark letter—choosing the right words is a task that provides us with the means to permanently commemorate someone we knew or loved, and to give sympathy and healing to those left behind. Close family and friends will read and re-read letters of condolence, and keep them as precious testimonies to their beloved. This section offers guidance on what to write and how to phrase it.

words of comfort

For most people, sending a letter of condolence is done rarely, so finding the best ways to express yourself is doubly challenging; indeed, many people don't write at all as they struggle to cope with a bereavement. But expressing yourself can help ease the pain, and since your letter acts as a memorial to honor the deceased, it will have extra value.

As with most important things in life, certain elements of formality should be observed for the letter. It should, ideally, be handwritten on plain,

headed paper, although cards and notes are also entirely acceptable. Your letter does not have to be too long—bear in mind the emotional vulnerability of the recipient, and the fact that they will probably be dealing with many unwelcome practicalities. But take your time choosing your exact words and phrases; respect your feelings, your memories of the deceased, and focus on the comfort you are trying to communicate to their nearest and dearest. While generally letters are sent around the time of the funeral, many of the bereaved find that the months after a funeral, when all immediate support has stopped, can be a painful time and it is then that a letter is the most welcome.

opening the letter

Always write to the nearest relation—husband, wife, or eldest child. Begin by expressing your sorrow at the loss. (For example: **"I was so sorry to hear of the death of your..."**) If the death was a shock, you can say so, while if the person had been sick for some time, you could refer to that by saying they are no longer suffering.

Be careful of descriptive terms: **"loss"** and **"death"** are acceptable, but stay away from anything sharper, particularly if the death was sudden or tragic. By contrast, some people don't like euphemisms such as **"passing on"** or **"passing over"**; imagine yourself as the recipient, and judge accordingly.

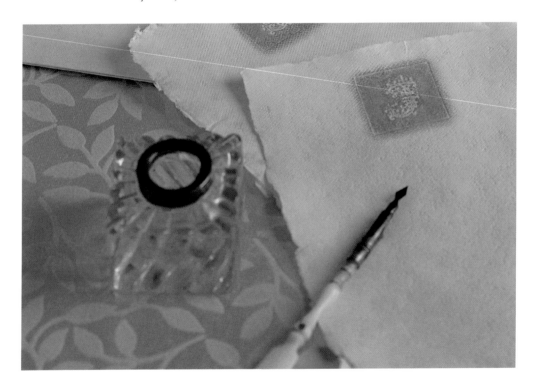

expressing yourself

As you describe your memories of the deceased, don't feel hampered by not "saying the right thing." If your letter is genuine, it will be entirely right. And, although this is not the time for the unvarnished truth, personal and even trivial recollections, when they are sincere, are exactly what make it strongest.

If you are finding recollections hard to write, speak them out loud; then write what you have said down. This gives your letter a smooth flow. Recall happy meetings, great parties, and the deceased's achievements as they affected you. Whether it was their delicious fruitcake, career leadership, or inspired and merry friendship, explain how they improved your life. Each sentence should be a genuine compliment. Describe your relationship with the deceased and how you felt about them—list their qualities and explain what you will miss most about them.

the tribute

As you pay your respects, ask yourself what the deceased gave the world and the people around them. If they were precious to you, don't feel embarrassed to say so. List their unique strengths and achievements and give specific details of how and why they were appreciated

by those who knew them. If you had a difficult relationship with the deceased at any time, you could use the phrase **"a great character."** If you were aware of any friction within their family, remember that however much the mourners may have grumbled in the person's lifetime, they may be having second thoughts. And even if they are not, it is not up to you to point this out—keep your tribute true, but not all-encompassing.

offering consolation

Put yourself in the mourner's position. Explain that, while you may not be able to understand what they are going through, you wish to express your sympathy for the loss, shock, and strain. Mention you knew how much the deceased loved them—give an example or a recollection, if you can. Make an offer of practical help; while it may not be taken up, it should be sincerely made.

Offer words of comfort. It is probably easier here to list what not to write rather than what you may say. Avoid suggesting they **"get over it"** or that the death **"was God's will,"** as well as any mention of the possibility that the departed is "**better off dead.**" While always produced with the best of intentions, these brisk sentiments tend to be both cliched and unhelpful. If you are writing following the loss of a colleague, you are representative of your firm so you should take care to avoid endless religious statements that might not be appropriate.

Simply express your understanding that the death of the deceased must be felt as a huge loss to everyone, but that the mourner must be grieving the most. If you have lived through a bereavement of your own, the mourner may find it useful to hear how you began to cope and heal. Offer your heartfelt sympathy and, if you can, companionship in the weeks that follow the funeral.

ending the letter

Extend your sympathies to other family and friends, and pass on a further offer of practical, everyday help. Remind the mourner that they are in your thoughts or prayers. If you write after attending the funeral, include a note about how the departed would have appreciated the ceremony or the wake.

Don't expect a response to your letter; it is not customary and the mourners will be besieged by practicalities that may prevent them from answering letters.

LETTER OF CONDOLENCE

This is, of course, a very personal letter to write, but there should be three key elements: your memories of, and relationship with, the deceased; your tribute to their character; and finally, your consolation of the bereaved. Ordering the letter in this way not only conforms to good manners, but can also help you to arrange your thoughts.

SAMPLE CONDOLENCE LETTER
This template provides a guide to phrases you might use in your letter, as well as a structure and inspiration for its content.

[date]

Dear _____

I thought I would write to you to express my sympathy for the death of [name of deceased]./ I was so sorry to hear about your loss/the death of [name of deceased].

[if you have heard of the death from a third party:] It was with great sadness that I learned about the death of [name of deceased].

[if you are writing about the death of a colleague:] I am writing on behalf of the friends and colleagues of [name of deceased] at [organization] to express our sympathy at the death of [name of deceased].

Everyone at work/in the family joins me in sending our deepest sympathy for your loss.

[name of deceased] was a great friend/colleague/relation to me. [explain why]
One of our happiest times was [give details]. He/she will be sadly missed. [again, explain why]

He/she was [name unique qualities, strengths, and finest moments].
[pay tribute to career and family achievements]

[express sympathy with words of comfort]

Please let me know if you need anything—or if I can drop by with anything you need in the next few weeks.

As ever, I/we all send you our deepest condolences and great sympathy for you. You are in my thoughts and prayers.

Love/With deepest sympathy/Sincerely,

[signature]

FORMAL LETTERS OF CONDOLENCE

If you don't know the bereaved intimately, these respectful, but empathetic, templates might be more appropriate.

FORMAL CONDOLENCE LETTERS
The template above is suitable if you have heard of the death through a third party, but still wish to pay tribute to the deceased. The template to the right has a more formal style, and is suitable for those with whom you had a long-standing or family connection but did not know well.

Dear _____

I cannot find the words to say how saddened we were to hear of the loss of [deceased's name].

I understand that, at the moment, you wish to be alone with your family and close friends but although I do not want to disturb you with a telephone call, I wanted you to know that we are all thinking of you.

Please feel free to ask me if there is anything I can do to help you at the moment.

Sincerely,

[signature]

Dear _____

It was with enormous sadness that we heard that [deceased's name], your dear [their relationship to the mourner], and our wonderful [friend/aunt/uncle/cousin, as appropriate] is no longer with us.

We understand how desolate you must be feeling and we regret that we did not see as much of [deceased's name] in recent years as we would have liked. We have wonderful memories of the occasions when we were able to meet.

You can be very proud of having had such a [friend/mother/husband/partner] and we will never forget his/her remarkable [include an individual characteristic, e.g., overwhelming kindness/infectious laugh].

Sincerely,

[signature]

LETTERS OF REQUEST
how to get what you want

Asking for what you want is not easy for many people, particularly the more socially diffident among us. No one wants to be seen as pushy or to have an out-of-proportion "sense of entitlement," but equally we all need, and deserve, help from others. Whether you need a favor, some assistance with family or friends, or a helping hand with your career, the perfect, and most socially adept, way to ask for what you want is by letter.

how to get what you want in writing

When you write a letter of request, you can refine the wording to make your request crystal clear—avoiding fluffing your lines nervously on the phone—while the recipient will be grateful to be given the time and space to consider your request, and may be more likely to grant it. And for those still hesitating, any natural feelings of delicacy can be put to good use by including phrases of tact and *politesse*, which are essential to a letter of request. Follow these guidelines to produce an effective letter.

Keep your letter as concise as possible. You don't need to be brief, but do not burden the reader with unnecessary detail. For example, if you are asking for a letter of recommendation for a job, explain the role and what it involves, but do not include pages of rhapsodies on why you want it—a sentence or two will do. However, it is often said that in professional fundraising, a longer letter gets a better response.

The tone of your letter should be bright, cheerful, and polite. If, for instance, you are begging your neighbors to keep their saxophone practice to daylight hours, do not write the letter when you are sleep-deprived and irritable, if possible. However annoying it may be, staying courteous under pressure can produce a positive "mirror response." If the letter is awkward and you are unsure whether you have achieved a polite tone, it is best to ask someone else to read and comment on your draft before you mail it.

Be clear about what you want, by when, and how. You could draft your points first on scrap paper. For instance, if you need a ride to a distant wedding or reunion, suggest a meeting point for you both, and ask them to let you know if they can help by a certain date—well in time for you to order a discount train ticket if they can't. You should aim to make your request easy to fulfill: if, for example, you want your reader to bring a dish of food to a party, specify that you would like a dessert that feeds five people. If you want them to send you something in the mail, include your address and stamps.

Don't apologize for your request. If it is reasonable, there is no need—a touch of flattery of your recipient should produce much better results. (However, it goes without saying that emotional manipulation is worthy of neither of you.) And you should make sure that you show your reader the benefits of your request. For instance, if you are asking for some leeway for your elderly mother who is staying with you, express your hope that quiet time for her will mean she enjoys her vacation with the family even more.

Keep your letter personal, complimentary, and address the recipient directly. Remember to ask the recipient to get in touch with you about any questions and remind them of your contact details. A good tactic, if you can, is to offer something in return.

Ensure that you thank them for considering your request. If appropriate, you could offer to follow up the letter with a phonecall.

writing a fundraising letter

Keep the page layout airy—i.e., include white space in the margin, and keep sentences and paragraphs short for maximum readability. In terms of style, use active sentences rather than passive verbs, and avoid jargon and in-house terms—donors won't understand, or care, about them.

Address each potential donor by name, and subsequently as "you" throughout. Speak to readers clearly and specifically by making sure each sentence makes your case. For example, rather than writing, **"The Green Neighborhood project was set up to aid the block's carbon footprint,"** include the more lively, sharper point: **"Last year, our Green Neighborhood project raised enough to plant 50 new trees in Brazil."**

Focus on the outcome of your current campaign, not on the internal details of how your organization works. For instance: **"The small, but growing, Brazilian forest provides enough oxygen to reduce the pollution of over half the cars on our block."** Try also to appeal to readers' hearts and minds, but don't be over-emotional or use hype. The best approach is to keep it human—for example, by using quotations and case studies—and to

add credibility by using testimonials where you can do this.

Always include the benefits of the reader's potential donation, not just the feature. For example, **"Each batch of your cupcakes could raise $20"** is helpful, but **"At the last bake sale, our delicious cupcakes sold in moments and made $50. Each $20 buys a new sapling"** is much stronger.

Most importantly, remember to include the legal requirements a fundraising letter needs. These vary and it is essential to seek professional advice before you start. In the US, requirements and procedures vary from state to state. In the UK, as a minimum, you must list your charity registration number and your company registration (if you are incorporated), as well as your registered address—The Institute of Fundraising and The Charity Commission offer guidelines, but you must get your correspondence professionally checked by legal advisers.

LETTERS OF REQUEST

Whether your request is large or small, the rules remain the same: courtesy, clarity, and, if the request is tricky, calm. The same rules apply to the professional version of these letters too.

Dear ["Neighbor" or neighbor's name],

As our hours don't usually overlap and we rarely meet by chance, I thought I would write to you to ask for a little understanding. As you probably know, I have a long commute to work and must get up very early each morning and, of course, this means I must go to bed early each evening. Your hours, I have noticed, are very different to mine and this is causing me a little difficulty.

The walls of our home are very thin and we are all forced to participate, to some extent, in our neighbors' lives. Therefore, I hope you will understand if I ask you to turn your television and music down after 10pm so that I can sleep easily.

Thanking you for your kindness. / Many thanks for your understanding on this matter. / With many thanks,

Sincerely,

[signature]

Dear [neighbor's name],

I know that children of [name of their child]'s age can be very lively and it is extremely difficult to keep them still, but I have just planted some new beds and am hoping for a really wonderful display of flowers in a few months' time.

I would therefore be grateful if you could ask your children if they could try very hard not to throw their baseball into my garden. I promise to give you a lovely bunch of flowers in the summer if I manage to grow them without any accidents.

Sincerely,

[signature]

LETTERS TO NEIGHBORS
The templates here give examples of writing "awkward" letters to neighbors, which tend to be the most difficult ones to create.

AWKWARD SITUATIONS
the best strategies

Whatever the cause of a difficult situation, the advantage of taking action in writing is that producing a letter helps you calm down. Unlike other communications, such as a phone call or a hasty email, laying out the problem clearly and in your own time allows you to plan exactly what you need to say and to choose the tone that will promote the best response.

how to approach complaints and apologies

An effective letter is concise and credible, and sticks to the facts. If you are writing a letter of complaint, begin by checking your rights. For example, consumer laws vary from country to country and from state to state. If the matter is serious, remember these tips are not a substitute for legal advice, which you will need. Always obtain professional advice and guidance—your first port of call could be your central or regional government authorities, or the relevant trade association or regulatory body. Then, find the right person to write to—check the full name and, if necessary, include their correct job title. Keep a firm bright tone throughout: if you are complaining, don't be tempted to drift into sarcasm, or, if apologizing, to be over-emotional.

Start by explaining the problem from your point of view: list any action you have taken so far, name whomever you dealt with, and the results. You should include the events that caused the problem and any relevant circumstances. State the damage or inconvenience the problem created; if you caused it, don't underestimate it.

If appropriate, name a date by which you expect a reply and follow up if it doesn't arrive, whether by phone or further correspondence. For complaints, consider whether a reminder letter will be worthwhile. In an organization, refer the matter upwards. If you are writing an apology, you should check that the letter has been received, but not press for instant forgiveness. Always keep a copy of the letter for your own reference.

LETTERS OF APOLOGY

Simple, sincere apologies work best. Most importantly, your letter should be constructive—always suggest a solution that the recipient will be happy with, and one which means you can kiss goodbye to the problem.

Dear [name]

I feel awful about [name of child]'s behavior at your house yesterday afternoon. He/she has always been a very lively child, but he/she rarely becomes that excited—certainly not to the extent that he/she completely forgets his/her manners.

Please excuse the mess he/she caused on this occasion and, above all, his/her breaking your lovely dish. I hope you are able to accept my offer to buy a replacement as it would make me feel much happier about the damage he/she caused.

Sincerely,

[signature]

Dear ["Neighbor" or neighbor's name]

I feel I should apologize for the noise that my guests and I made last night and the disturbance it caused you. A dear friend was moving away—we were wishing him farewell and did not realize how late it was nor that we were being over-enthusiastic in our celebrations.

I should have forewarned you of the party but it slipped my mind. Once again, please forgive me for the annoyance.

Sincerely,

[signature]

APOLOGY LETTERS
You may need to apologize on behalf of your child at some point—follow the style of the template above to do this. Or, if you have offended a neighbor, even if only accidentally, writing a letter of apology in the style of the template on the left is a good way to smooth things over.

LETTERS OF COMPLAINT

Complaints are best made with confidence—once you have checked your rights, "I am entitled to" is stronger and clearer than "I think I am entitled to."

BUSINESS LETTER OF COMPLAINT

Use this template to plan a letter to complain for poor or faulty products or service. Remember not to send originals of receipts or sales vouchers, only photocopies, and to keep a copy of your letter.

[your address and contact details]

[name, business name, and address of trader]

[date]

Dear [name of trader],

[your reference number, as appropriate]

[your account number, as appropriate]

[product reference or model number, as appropriate]

On [date], you supplied and fitted/I bought from you [product/service, for example: new decking to the area behind my property/a new armchair], for which I paid you [$/£ sum]. I have now discovered the [product/service] is faulty.

The problems are: [list if more than one, for example: the timber is warping; the cover has ripped]

On [date], I rang your customer complaints department, explained the product was faulty, and gave the operator [include name if possible] my details.

I have not heard from you, and now request delivery of a replacement [product, in the same style/color/model]/I wish to claim a free repair and replacement.

I look forward to hearing from you within the next ten days.

Sincerely,

[signature]

Enc: [receipt—photocopy only]

A THANK-YOU LETTER
the art of being grateful

Why are thank-you letters so difficult to write? After a great day out, or the first time you use a wonderful gift, your letter should write itself. But the best of us can struggle to find the right words. This chapter will help you produce personal, lasting, and creative ways to say thank you. Templates are included, too, for professional thanks, such as for a charity donation or local church work.

the importance of saying thank you

A tradition for centuries, the thank-you letter gives joy to the recipient as barely any other communication does. In some ways, we now live in a world without letters, where texting and emailing have taken over our lives. According to a survey in the early 2000s, a third of people aged under 35 have never written to a loved one. And for everyone today, mail means reminders, bills, or just junk. Yet a handwritten card or letter starts an ordinary day with enjoyment and interest.

While not as formal or as rule-bound as business communications or invitations, it is a common misconception that thank-you letters are the preserve of the older generation. Princess Diana was known—and admired—for her great skill and speed at writing thank-you letters. Internet forums worldwide bear witness to the efforts of mothers to coax their young into the first stumbling attempts to say thank you.

Do we roll with the latest fashions and satisfy ourselves with a quick text or a one-line email, which at least are an acknowledgment? Those of us who write know that we all get more pleasure from receiving a proper letter in the mail. As a bonus, a letter lasts forever as a tangible, expressive piece of affection.

We know too, that just as we might tell our children, saying thank you is a key life skill—it's a way to value others, and nothing could be more important than that. The Milanese St Ambrose wrote, "No duty is more urgent than that of returning thanks." And gratitude is good for us too—appreciating what we have and are given is a tried-and-tested means to personal happiness. Writing a thank-you letter, choosing the paper, and picking the words focuses your thoughts and strengthens your happy memories of the event or what you have been given; and the finished piece is a small gift of thanks in return for the joy you have been given.

personal thank-yous

The key to a successful thank-you letter is making it personal—for you and the recipient. Always explain why you have enjoyed something. Your letter does not have to be long: etiquette expert Debrett's suggests it should be "warm, witty, and to the point."

You can use cards, notelets, and home-made stationery for your letter, but the classic thank-you is sent on plain headed paper (see pages 144–6). Don't include the date or your address on a card; if you are sending a postcard, then you can leave out the salutation too.

THANK-YOU LETTER FOR A GIFT

When writing a personal thank-you letter, standard templates may not at first seem the best place to start, but the framework provided here lays out a comprehensive series of options for you to complete with your individual recollections and thoughts.

GIFT THANK-YOU LETTER
Follow this general wording, adding in personal details, to thank someone for a gift you have received.

[address]

[date]

Dear *[name of recipient, e.g., Fred, Aunt June, Grandpa, etc.]*

Thank you very much for the _____. It was a lovely surprise and I have already used it when I _____.

It looks great as part of my collection/the collection I have decided to start/in the living room/my bedroom/with the rest of my wardrobe, etc.
It will be a great help when _____.
It cheered me up after _____.
I will save it for "best" when _____.
I love/enjoy/appreciate it particularly because _____.
Every time I use/read/wear the _____, I will remember your thoughtfulness—how clever of you to find it.
At Christmas/on my birthday I/we *[include details of festivities]*.

I hope you are *[all]* well—it would be great to know how you are.
[enquire after health of spouse/children/pets—referring to when you last saw them]

[enquire after recipient's job/schooling/recent life event]

Thank you so much again for your generosity. Love to you and *[name other family members]*,

Love/Best Love/Yours,

Thank-you Letter for Hospitality

In days of yore, thanks for hospitality were always addressed to the lady of the house—women reigned in the worlds of family and society—but, with the enthusiastic entry of menfolk into the kitchen, it seems a bit churlish to exclude thanks to the cook. The abiding rule is to be polite—so address your letter to the named host or both halves of a couple, or, if in doubt, the half who did the most work.

Dear _____

Thank you very much for inviting us to _____.

We had a lovely time because _____.
I particularly enjoyed the _____ [name a dish], as [give reason].
How clever of you to choose [name dish/theme/other guests] to create such a fine mix for a day/evening/weekend.
I so enjoyed seeing _____ again/meeting _____ because [give reason].
We all laughed when [recount funniest moment].

Your house/garden/flat looked wonderful—I do admire your [name feature and explain].

I hope you have recovered after such a lot of work—it was much appreciated by all. [enquire after recent health of spouse/children/pets]

Thank you so much again for your generosity. You must come and see us soon. Love to you and [name others].

Love/Best Love/Yours,

HOSPITALITY THANK-YOU LETTER
Use this template to thank someone after a dinner party or other social event that they have arranged.

ways to make your letter personal

Firstly, write promptly. This means: the day after a dinner party; in the week after Christmas or a birthday; the week following a wedding or Bar Mitzvah. However, as the writer Francis Bacon wrote: "late thanks are ever best"—a tardy letter shows the event or parcel made a strong impression.

If you have one, use a fountain pen. Real ink makes a difference—ballpoint, although ubiquitous, doesn't do either of you justice. And never type a personal letter sent through the mail.

Stay clear of expressing ecstasy or slavish adoration, particularly for mundane contributions to the household: "The tea cloth is perfectly exquisite! I appreciate your lovely gift more than I can say, both for its own sake and for your kindness. . ." may have worked for Emily Post, but smacks of overdoing it in our cynical times. However, be specific. **"Great food"** is well-meaning but bland; **"The squirrel pie was delicious"** is more memorable. Your letter should be unique to the recipient, and to you. Also, never describe any gift or experience as **"unusual,"** and be careful of **"memorable," "infinite,"** or **"enduring."** For gifts of money, you should refer briefly to **"the generous check"** and detail how you spent it: according to Debrett's, thanks for gifts of money should "never mention the quantity."

Compliments about personal appearance, providing they focus on face or clothing, are always acceptable. In the same way, praise for the host's children, or animals, can be a welcome addition. Again, stay clear of ambiguous phrases: even besotted parents understand that a child labeled a "free spirit" is likely to end up in jail, while, in our diet-conscious times, no one wants their beloved pet damned as **"cuddly." "Intelligent," "sweet-natured," "heart-melting,"** and **"great company"** are fine for both.

Assuming your friends are trustworthy, feel free to indulge in a touch of gossip—be indiscreet, but not snarky. **"Wonderful food, Lola looked fabulous—but I thought Steve had aged"** is probably OK; **"Wonderful food, shame I couldn't eat it because Steve's denture problem made me nauseous"** is too much information. Save any particularly spiky observations for a phonecall, or your written words may come back to haunt you.

Finish your letter with renewed thanks and warm regards to everyone in the household by name, and a personal sign-off to the host or giver.

how to be grateful for a disaster

While your letter writes itself for an event or gift you loved, creating authentic correspondence for an unwanted or insensitive gift—hair-removal kit, anyone?—can be a challenge. Staff at Debrett's explain that not liking something is "irrelevant" to your thanks—these tips will help you stay honest, but kind.

Remember your job is to gratify the giver or the host: you can always find something pleasant to say. If you have received a terrible present, skim over the offending object with a phrase of simple thanks and reassurance that it will be **"useful"** or **"valued,"** and change the subject briskly.

Bear in mind that many of the worst gifts have been given with the best of motives. Receiving a gift that is too intimate—for example, a self-help book on the menopause before the age of 50—can be difficult, because it has clearly been picked kindly and thoughtfully. Deal with the sting by thanking the giver for their thoughtfulness and alertness to your needs: **"How kind of you to take an interest in my health as the years roll by"**—then reward yourself by binning it. Also, no kindly giver wants to know if the gift went wrong. If, for example, you erupted in hives after receiving costume jewelry, paint clear nail varnish over the metal or give it to a thrift store—pointing it out can make you look ungrateful or greedy.

If, in your opinion, you have sent an extremely expensive gift and received, frankly, not enough in return, ignore it; your giver will no doubt have noticed and make it up to you next time.

In the case of a social event having gone awry, choose your words carefully. If a meal was awful, reserve your compliments for another part of the occasion. Try praising the choice of guests, the décor, the music, and, as a failsafe, the hostess's appearance. Small catering disasters—such as finding your host's dog in the kitchen licking its lips after the chocolate cake has disappeared—can be turned into a funny story. Your host, after all, is entertaining you, no matter how accidentally. Similarly, should other guests make a scene, or if there was a wounding argument at the table, you can major on the "drama" of the occasion—by thanking your hosts for **"allowing you into their lives."** However, avoid double-edged compliments; only you will think they are funny, which is not enough, given that someone else apart from the recipient may read the letter.

If you find it particularly hard to think of things to compliment, make your own card and illustrate it with a drawing or a photo—this stays personal, but avoids articulating feelings of gratitude. Of course, if words still fail you, you could invite the recipient back to your home as a kindly gesture.

children's thank-you letters

A grounding in good manners is equipment for life; learning to say thank you is pretty basic, and, while it can be difficult for small children to understand, brings advantages to them that can one day stretch far beyond their first etchings over a paint-stained notelet. This section shows you how to coax a child into his or her first endeavors of self-expression, and also offers ideas on how to get the very young into the habit of saying thank you.

In the early 21st century, one of Britain's top public schools, Wellington College, Berkshire, introduced "courtesy lessons." Headmaster Anthony Seldom explained that his young charges were not fit for the world of modern business and commerce without good manners. Many parents agree—while texts and emails are seen as thanks enough for many, others see that a letter makes more of an impression and gives pleasure and reward to writer and reader alike.

Nothing beats the charm of a child's letter:

"Darrling Granna thank you for my truck. How is Mr Silky I hope his tale is fixed yours Oli ps come and stay now"

It may not be a Pulitzer winner, but its sincerity, directness, and firm focus are equally enduring.

the thankless task:

Ten phrases that persuade a child to write thank-you letters

Given that the prospect of writing even a word of gratitude for a rapture-inducing toy makes even the most charming child slump into hopeless illiteracy, you may need help. The irritating truths and motivations below are also suitable to spur on reluctant adults (by which I mean men).

1. "It gets me off your back. In this world, actions (or lack of them) have consequences. I am one of them."
2. "Good manners cost nothing."
3. "You will be proud of yourself."
4. "No, you are not saving trees. You are hurting Granny's feelings."
5. "Granny will love it." (no matter how bad it is)
6. "Granny wants to know what you are doing in life—letters are a good way to keep in touch with the family."
7. "Granny needs to know if you have received it. We are not paying for a long-distance call."
8. "You may receive a better gift next year if you are kind to the person who was kind to you."
9. "You may receive no gift next year if you fail to write a thank-you letter."
10. "Should you ever become famous, your letter might be published." (Winston Churchill's juvenile outpourings were, if anyone asks.)

Finally, including a decent pen or a pack of small notecards in their Christmas stocking, or as an extra birthday gift, should make the point.

ideas for young children's thank-you cards

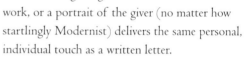

If your child is really too young to write much, they can still send wonderful, personal cards to friends and family using these simple craft ideas.

Fold A5-sized plain white cardstock into cards and ask your child to put a painted handprint on it before you or he/she writes a note inside. If you wish to write a thank-you for a baby's gift, you can send cards with footprints.

Another option, again using a blank card, is to stick a photograph of your child opening his/her presents on the front; a short note, or even just the child's name, will be hugely augmented by the photo that shows the expressions on their faces. Similarly, simply glue a recent photograph to the front of a blank postcard and leave space for the child to sign his/her name at the bottom.

You could also ask your child to draw his/her thank-you letter—a sketch showing the gift at work, or a portrait of the giver (no matter how startlingly Modernist) delivers the same personal, individual touch as a written letter.

If your child is thanking another child—say for a party gift—you can send a group picture of all the party guests as the front of a card, or, if you have planned your etiquette in advance, a photograph of each child. Include a short, but individual, thank you signed by your child. Young children who cannot read will appreciate and understand the card (and learn how nice thank-yous are pleasingly early in life).

professional thank-you letter

Thank-you letters are not just the preserve of family and friends. Many people in the world of work need to thank others for corporate social occasions—for example, after a seasonal lunch, a day out, or business entertainment. Just as how you dress and behave at work reflects your personal business brand, so your letter showcases your individual skills. Your stationery may be corporate, and your correspondence should certainly reflect your abilities as a worthy representative of your organization, but the words you choose to use provide you with an additional opportunity to shine.

the seven golden rules of writing professional thank-you letters

1. Write promptly—ideally, within 24 hours of the occasion—and use company letterhead paper. Typed letters and emails are fine.
2. Address your letter to the person who invited you (not literally—their PA will not be expecting it), or, failing that, the most senior member of the group.
3. Keep the tone light, brief, and personal, but professional. Detail what you enjoyed, and why.
4. Thank the host for the chance to meet new faces in the business/to catch up with old friends. Also express your thanks and appreciation for the occasion, and the recipients' time.

5. If you are sending thanks for an informal interview, briefly reiterate your most relevant skills and experience for the job. If you are thanking someone for an informal meeting or lunch, sum up the conclusion of the meeting, referring to a separate document for any business issues raised.
6. Mention any extra details you may have forgotten at the time, and repeat your enthusiasm and interest for either the job or for the projects you are working on together.
7. Include your contact details, reiterate your thanks, and sign off; keeping it brief is always polite in a busy professional world.

PROFESSIONAL THANK-YOU LETTER

Sending a well-written thank-you letter is an excellent way to make a favorable impression on a potential or current boss. For interviewees, it demonstrates that you can express yourself in writing, and between companies it suggests knowledge of good manners and can encourage a business relationship to flourish.

THANK-YOU LETTER FOR WORK SITUATIONS
This template can be adapted and used by a job applicant or after a work event, such as a meeting or formal dinner.

[your name and address]
[host/hostess's name]
[full business title]
[business name in full]
[address]
[date]

Dear [name of host/hostess],

I thought I would drop you a line to thank you for sparing the time to meet me yesterday/the chance to be interviewed for the position of [name in full of vacancy]/the wonderful time we had at your annual celebrations yesterday.

It was a pleasure to see/meet you. I particularly enjoyed catching up with [name mutual associates] and getting the news on your current projects and challenges.

[for interviewees:] I confirm my interest in the position and would like to become a part of the [company name] team. The job holds many opportunities—and I believe my skills in [name] and qualifications could be an asset to you.

[for colleagues:] The [name of] projects sound very rewarding—working on it/them would be great for the company.

Don't hesitate to contact me at [telephone] or [email] if you need any additional information.

Thanks again for your time and consideration.

Sincerely,

[signature]

charity and fundraising thank-you letter

Thanking your donors personally is vital to the success of any community organization, yet somehow the task can fall by the wayside. Showing thanks as well as appreciation is essential—your givers will want to know how their donations are being spent. And, as a way to maintain the interest of committed and regular donors, your letter can also become an essential marketing tool. Several giving surveys reveal that the speed of response to a gift increases the chances of getting further, larger donations in future.

making your fundraising thank-you letter more effective

Keep it professional—use a letterhead, and do not plaster your letter with logos or bright colors. Your letter should reinforce the credibility of your cause. You should send it from the most senior person in your organization, or the Head of Donations. Similarly, address your letter to the most senior person involved in the giving; for example, if you are thanking a school, address it to the head teacher or principal. Make it personal—a typewritten letter is fine, but avoid obvious photocopies, and, if you can, handwrite the salutation and sign it in ink.

Unlike a social thank-you letter, include a specific mention of the sum; this also acts as a receipt for tax. Then, if your donor has given time and effort, list the tasks they did to help. Remember that your donor is your partner in a shared endeavor—treat them as such with plenty of information about how the community organization is doing as a whole.

You should then explain how your organization has benefited from their help. Say what their donation achieved, in detail. Make your description as tangible, and lively, as possible. Include case studies if you can—for instance, the gift of a water pump to an African village could be illustrated with stories about the village's healthy and happy mothers and children.

It is wise to time the letter for the end of the financial year, if possible, and to point out any tax breaks your donor may get, or can apply for, on behalf of themselves or your organization. However, save campaigning, or asking for more help, until you next get in touch—this letter is purely a courtesy.

[your name, organization, and address]

[name of donor]
[full business/organization title]
[business/organization name in full]
[address]

[date]

Dear _____.

I am writing to thank you for so kindly/generously supporting [my/our cause/fundraiser]. We were delighted to receive your help with [for example, leafleting or providing refreshments]/your generous gift of $/£ [insert sum].

Every gift we receive is important. Our campaign/event has raised $/£ [insert sum] for [name of cause]. Your donation, and those of other sponsors, was essential to our cause. Without your assistance, [I/we] would not have been able to provide the help we do to [outline cause—for example, local church work, helping the underprivileged/animals/the sick].

Your help/donation will now be put towards [detail help provided; include real examples of how someone has benefited, if possible, with names or a case study].

[insert news about your recent activities, if appropriate]

If you need more information, or have any questions, don't hesitate to get in touch with [me/us] on [telephone] or via [email].

I would like to thank you once again for your generosity and continued support, which is greatly appreciated.

Yours sincerely,

[your signature]
[your name]
[position in organization]

CHARITY THANK-YOU LETTER

For any community organization, maintaining contact with its donors is vital to its success. Writing a letter to thank them for their help will always be appreciated.

WORDING OF A CHARITY THANK-YOU LETTER
Following this template for a charity or fundraising thank-you letter will give a good impression and encourage the donor to support your organization in future.

CHAPTER 3

Love Letters

While it is easy to fall in love, we all know how tricky it can be to express it. This chapter explains how to tackle the most delicate of subjects: our own tender feelings. Using the love letters, quotes, and reminiscences of great lovers through the ages, as well as practical hints, you can learn how to create a letter that represents your feelings at their best, and fans the flames of love in the heart of the recipient.

A LOVE LETTER

words of love

For centuries, men and women have used the love letter to forge, maintain, and celebrate one of life's greatest gifts: romantic love. More powerful than most other forms of writing, a love letter can be intimate or flirtatious, soul-baring or hilarious, tender or provocative—but always potent and magical.

a lost art

Until the 20th century, couples routinely wrote love letters to further a romance—even the illiterate used local letter-writers or scribes to capture their sentiments for a beloved. And today, while the death of letter-writing is lamented in some circles, no loss is mourned more greatly than the lost art of the love letter.

Why is this? It seems that, unique among communications, not only does a love letter honor a relationship, and frame it for posterity, but the best actually improve and grow the love between a couple. In a love letter, love, passion, respect, tenderness, and sensuality become tangible—the uncertainty of abstract sentiment

is removed, replaced with love in physical form. And if you or your suitor is timid, or you have difficulty expressing the most intimate of feelings, a love letter will draw out, reveal, and enshrine the secrets of the heart.

Unlike the fleeting electronic moment of an email or a text, a written letter can be kept forever. Delivering joy to the recipient on arrival, every letter is a permanent declaration of love, an enduring testimony to a relationship. Evoking the same tenderness from writer and reader every time it is read, its magic does not fade over time. The key to writing a good love letter is releasing your heart to sing—and then capturing it.

the seven golden rules for writing a love letter

1. Choose your salutation. Ignore everyday greetings—"Hi", "Dear," and "Yo" don't set the right atmosphere. Use words of love, but be sincere; be light-hearted if necessary, and don't be scared to use pet names. "Dearest" and "Darling" may be cliches, but they create the tone you need.

2. Explain how you feel about your beloved. Don't feel under pressure—start with a draft, and read paragraphs aloud as you complete them so you can see how they sound.

3. Stick to tried and trusted techniques of self-examination—honesty, sincerity, and, vitally, memory. Starting with the time you were last together, recall how you felt. At first, don't think about your emotions. Instead—what were you doing? How did you feel physically? How did he/she move you? Then focus on how your heart and mind were behaving. Prosaic as it may sound, list your feelings as words. Once you feel you have recollected the experience, move onto the first time you met your partner—then choose another special time together. You now have the body of your letter—the feelings you have, expressed and framed; commit them to paper.

4. Be fresh, honest, and comfortable with your own voice. Don't be too shy to include what you love about them, no matter how quirky it may sound. What character traits draw you to them? What about the physical package? What makes you laugh? What makes you melt?

5. End by considering these points. What made you fall in love? What changed to make you realize you now love them more? How have you relied on them in the bad times, as well as the good? What thrills you about the future? What do you see in your vision of your life as a couple? And why do you treasure your beloved?

6. If you have been together for years, remember that a love letter can revitalize and refresh any relationship, so include shared memories such as a special birthday or anniversary—and if you are in a new relationship, you could look forward to the times you'll share with your beloved in the years to come.

7. Sign off personally. Choose a phrase that means something to both of you, or take the opportunity to create one. "Best love, always," is a favorite of mine.

POIGNANT POETRY AND KILLER LINES

Use these phrases to help say what you feel—whether it is a declaration of love, a musing on the romantic nature of your relationship, to mourn a parting, or even to say goodbye.

MUSINGS ON LOVE
You could add one of these quotes to your letter if you're having trouble expressing yourself.

"For every beauty there is an eye somewhere to see it. For every truth there is an ear somewhere to hear it. For every love there is a heart somewhere to receive it."
Ivan Panin (1855–1942)

"Love cannot endure indifference. It needs to be wanted. Like a lamp, it needs to be fed out of the oil of another's heart, or its flame burns low."
Henry Ward Beecher (1813–1887)

"Since love grows within you, so beauty grows. For love is the beauty of the soul."
St Augustine (354–430)

"True love is eternal, infinite, and always like itself. It is equal and pure, without violent demonstrations: it is seen with white hairs and is always young in the heart."
Honoré de Balzac (1799–1850)

"It is not the perfect but the imperfect who need love."
Oscar Wilde (1854–1900)

"The human heart, at whatever age, opens to the heart that opens in return."
Maria Edgeworth (1768–1849)

HOW DOES HE OR SHE FEEL?
If you are testing the water with a new love, slip one of these hints into your letter to provoke a response from him/her.

> "Ever has it been that love knows not its own depth until the hour of separation."
> Kahlil Gibran (1883–1931)

> "This bud of love, by summer's ripening breath, may prove a beauteous flower when next we meet."
> William Shakespeare (1564–1616)

> "Only in the agony of parting do we look into the depths of love."
> George Eliot (1819–1880)

> "Parting is all we know of heaven and all we need of hell."
> Emily Dickinson (1830–1886)

THE PAIN OF PARTING
Separated from your lover? You might like to use one of these lines.

> "The hottest love has the coldest end."
> Socrates (470–399 BCE)

> "Being strong sometimes means being able to let go."
> Anonymous

> "It takes a moment to say hello, but an age to say goodbye."
> Anonymous

HOW TO SAY GOODBYE
When writing the last love letter, making use of one of these quotes might allow you to say more easily what you feel.

turn-offs: what not to write

Be passionate, but avoid intensity. Fashions in love letters change through the ages—French novelist's Victor Hugo's (1802–1885) description to his lady about their love as "two souls who have finally found [...] a union, fiery and pure as they themselves... a religion" would have been revered in bohemian circles in the 19th century as nothing less than good and proper feeling, but might seem a little scary today. Equally, contemporary phrases such as "Your butt and those jeans make me hot to trot," or simply, "I really, really want you," may stir unease in the object of your affections if you don't know them that well. Your aim is to gently fan the flames of passion in the heart of another, not convince them you are a stalker.

Keep it (reasonably) clean. While many people find erotic writing a sexy, fun addition to their relationship, remember you are writing a billet doux to your beloved, not pen pals with the editor of Readers' Wives. Apart from the possibility of causing offense, erotica is notoriously hard to write well—even best-selling novelists have been thought to subcontract explicit sex scenes to specialist "technical" writers. Bear in mind, too, that, however complimentary, many recipients simply will not respond to explicit writing; general appreciation of physical beauty is far more likely to provoke the reaction you want.

Praise, celebrate, and compliment your beloved—but stay honest. Don't say "I do howl with laughter whenever you tell your golf joke" when it bores you, because insincerity will show up—particularly when it is surrounded by declarations of soft, tender feelings. And if you have chosen well, there should be so much to praise you shouldn't need to pile on false flattery.

Bare your soul—but avoid navel-gazing. Writing is communication to another, not a chance to regurgitate every fleeting thought of a mundane day, or an endless opportunity to write about yourself. Austrian novelist Franz Kafka (1883–1924) signed off a love letter to his soulmate: "Did I think of signing myself *Dein* (yours)? No, nothing could be more false. No, I am forever fettered to myself, that's what I am, and that's what I must try to live with." While passionate, the affair ended as Kafka unconsciously predicted, and much to his regret he did end up "fettered" to himself—the girl fled. However fascinating one is, and, indeed, deserves to be, focus on communicating; a good letter should be a conversation you are holding on behalf of yourself and your beloved.

"To write a good love letter, you ought to begin without knowing what you mean to say, and to finish without knowing what you have written."

JEAN-JACQUES ROUSSEAU (1712–1778)

SAMPLE LOVE LETTERS

A love letter is, of course, a deeply personal piece of writing, so these examples are here not so much to provide templates, but rather to offer inspiration and a starting point.

My darling [lover's name],

It feels as if I have waited my whole life to meet someone like you, [lover's name]. I love your [smile/eyes/kindness], I love your [thoughtfulness/voice/smell], I even love your [forgetfulness/untidiness/grouchiness in the morning], but most of all I love you.

I love each and every moment that we spend together and spend the time that we are apart thinking of when we will meet again.

You have done so much for me. [give example] I'm not sure you realize how thankful I am to you, and how much I treasure each and every gesture you have made.

You have made my life complete, you have made my days sweet, you have made my dreams come true. Some day soon, we will be together always.

All my love,
[your name]

SOON WE'LL BE TOGETHER
Lovers whom have been parted may exchange a letter like the one above.

I YEARN FOR YOU
In the first flush of love, you might write something similar to this letter.

My beloved [lover's name],

When I woke up this morning and thought of you, I couldn't stop smiling——the people on the train, the people in my office, even the man at the coffee shop must all be wondering what's going on. And I want to tell them that it's you.

You make me so very happy. I wish we could spend every moment together but, when we are apart, all I have to do is think of your wonderful [smile / sense of humor / laugh] *and all disappointments simply vanish. You are the man/woman beyond my dreams.*

I cannot wait until we meet again. Sometimes I worry that we will have nothing to talk about since all I do is think of you, but then I can tell you properly how fantastic you are and how lucky I am.

I yearn for you——come and see me soon.
[your name]

Dear *[ex-lover's name]*,

This is not an easy letter to write and, sitting here thinking of what to tell you, I keep remembering all the good times we have shared together. But I think we both know that those memories belong very much in the past and that our relationship has not been working well for some time now. We don't seem to be able to talk or have fun like we used to and, as much as I care about you, I cannot see a future for us together. I would sooner we called time on our relationship and have the chance of holding onto those wonderful memories than see either of us become disappointed by the other.

I hope that we will be able to keep our close friendship. One of the things I have most admired about you is your loyalty and honesty, but I realize that could be painful for you and wishful thinking on my part. Thank you for the time we have had——I have learnt so much from you.

My fondest love,

[your name]

SAYING FAREWELL
Writing a letter might help you to part kindly from a lover.

INSPIRED BY GENIUS
famous love letters

Written by the greatest artists, rulers, and novelists of their time, these love letters—and their passion—have survived centuries. Find inspiration from these extraordinary and beautiful declarations of love, the feeling that even emperors know is more important than any other—and read the words of James Joyce, one of the 20th century's finest novelists, to remind you that, no matter how strong our feelings, we are all lost in love at times.

write to me

James Joyce (1882–1941) became the father of the modern novel, and he credited much of his success to Nora Barnacle, the girl with whom he eloped from Dublin and whom he writes to here (right). Nora was the muse he described as his "portable Ireland" and she, for her part, was known to support him with down-to-earth horse sense as well as providing the model for his flirty, sexy heroine Molly Bloom in Joyce's *Ulysses*. His words show that even the greatest writers might have

Will you write something to me? I hope you will. How am I to sign myself? I won't sign anything at all, because I don't know what to sign myself.

difficulty in finding the right words to express how much they care for someone.

the immortal beloved

German composer Ludwig van Beethoven (1770–1827) held a lifelong secret. Going through his papers and music after his death, a single love letter was found. After almost two hundred years, the identity of his love remains a mystery—Beethoven refers to her only as "my Immortal Beloved."

July 6, 1806

My angel, my all, my very self—only a few words today and at that with your pencil… Why this deep sorrow where necessity speaks—can our love endure except through sacrifices—except through not demanding everything—can you change it that you are not wholly mine, I not wholly thine?

Oh, God! look out into the beauties of nature and comfort yourself with that which must be— love demands everything and that very justly—that it is with me so far as you are concerned, and you with me. If we were wholly united you would feel the pain of it as little as I!

Now a quick change to things internal from things external. We shall surely see each other; moreover, I cannot communicate to you the observations I have made during the last few days touching my own life—if our hearts were always close together I would make none of the kind. My heart is full of many things to say to you—ah!—there are moments when I feel that speech is nothing after all—cheer up—remain my true, only treasure, my all as I am yours; the gods must send us the rest that which shall be best for us.

Your faithful

Ludwig

I belong to you

With a life by day as an insurance clerk in gloomy post-war Austria and a life by night creating masterpieces of surrealist literature, Franz Kafka (1883–1924) was largely unknown as a writer in his short life. At the age of 29, he met Felice Bauer: their passionate, but doomed, affair lasted five years. This letter, written the year they met, shows the strength and pain of Kafka's love in full force.

November 11, 1912

Fräulein Felice!

I am now going to ask you a favor which sounds quite crazy, and which I should regard as such, were I the one to receive the letter. It is also the very greatest test that even the kindest person could be put to. Well, this is it:

Write to me only once a week, so that your letter arrives on Sunday—for I cannot endure your daily letters, I am incapable of enduring them. For instance, I answer one of your letters, then lie in bed in apparent calm, but my heart beats through my entire body and is conscious only of you. I belong to you; there is really no other way of expressing it, and that is not strong enough...

Franz

August 15, 1846

I will cover you with love when next I see you, with caresses, with ecstasy. I want to gorge you with all the joys of the flesh, so that you faint and die.

I want you to be amazed by me, and to confess to yourself that you had never even dreamed of such transports...

When you are old, I want you to recall those few hours, I want your dry bones to quiver with joy when you think of them.

the marriage of love

French novelist Gustave Flaubert (1821–1880) sent this to his wife, Louise Colet, after they had been apart for some time. While Flaubert remains lauded for his celebrations of rebellious sensuality in his novels of 19th-century provincial life, none has the power of this short, private, and joyfully raunchy missive.

Paris, December, 1795

I wake filled with thoughts of you. Your portrait and the intoxicating evening that we spent yesterday have left my senses in turmoil. Sweet, incomparable Josephine, what a strange effect you have on my heart! Are you angry? Do I see you looking sad? Are you worried?... My soul aches with sorrow, and there can be no rest for your lover; but is there still more in store for me when, yielding to the profound feelings which overwhelm me, I draw from your lips, from your heart a love which consumes me with fire? Ah! it was last night that I fully realized how false an image of you your portrait gives!

You are leaving at noon; I shall see you in three hours.

Until then, mio dolce amor, a thousand kisses; but give me none in return, for they set my blood on fire.

love conquers all

Said to have written over 70,00 letters in his lifetime, French emperor Napoleon Bonaparte (1763–1821) wrote this letter to his Empress, Josephine, shortly before their marriage.

the priceless treasure

Father of the American novel, Mark Twain (1835–1910) addressed this short, but fervent and tender note to his fiancée, Olivia Langdon.

May 12, 1869

Out of the depths of my happy heart wells a great tide of love and prayer for this priceless treasure that is confided to my life-long keeping.

You cannot see its intangible waves as they flow towards you, darling, but in these lines you will hear, as it were, the distant beating of the surf.

MORE WORDS OF LOVE

Still struggling to find the right words to say what he or she means to you? These shorter sentiments may inspire you, too, as you write your love letter.

FURTHER WORDS OF LOVE
Use these quotes directly in your letter or just for inspiration.

"An astonishing quantity of kisses are flying about——the Deuce!——I see a whole crowd of them! ha! ha! I have just caught three——they are delicious!"
Wolfgang Amadeus Mozart to his wife, Constanzia (1756–1791)

"Away from you the world is a desert. You have taken more than my soul."
Napoleon (1763–1821) to Josephine

"I am always conscious of my nearness to you; your presence never leaves me."
Johann Wolfgang von Goethe (1749–1832)

"I love you——those three words have my life in them."
Tsaritsa Alexandra (1872–1918) to Nicholas II

"Love is the emblem of eternity: it confounds all notion of time: effaces all memory of a beginning, all fear of an end."
Madame de Staël (1766–1817)

love yourself too... a little warning

While your letter will be kept, and, ideally, treasured, be aware that there can be a downside to creating such permanent symbols of love. Once your most intimate sentiments are committed to writing, anyone can read them—as you will see in the case of these letters here. As well as rose-strewn writing paper or hand-decorated cards, remember this also applies to emails, faxes, and even text messages. If the relationship ends, you won't want your inner secrets and feelings broadcast to the world. So be careful—no matter how ardent your passion, save your finest feelings and words for those you trust. In any case, people you don't trust don't deserve them.

CHAPTER 4

Netiquette

Faced with the explosion in electronic communication over the last twenty years, it's no wonder that the majority of us find "netiquette"—writing rules for email, text, and social networking—something of a challenge. But the time-honored essentials of etiquette still apply, as do the key principles of good writing—clear communication and, equally, courtesy. This chapter shows you how to create correspondence for electronic media that reflects your good manners and shows your writing powers off to their best effect.

The Art of Email
communicating online

There are few of us today who can still avoid email, even if we want to, and those who use it everyday still find it tricky to choose the right wording, so this section provides special rules for writing for the electronic media, with the consideration for the reader that underlies both fine writing and good social skills. Screens are more difficult to read than paper, so you will find tips and tricks here to make your words flow more easily for your reader as well as impress them. You will find out, too, how to deal with one of the modern world's most delicate tasks—how to strike the right personal or professional note in the absence of face-to-face communication.

online correspondence

While the various means of communication— paper, computer, and cell screens—can each achieve superb results, each one produces different reader experiences, and the good web writer always takes account of this. Screen writing is more difficult to read than text on paper (unless your handwriting is really dreadful), so treat your reader with the respect they deserve and keep communications brief, particularly with professional emails. French philosopher Blaise Pascal wrote to a friend: "Forgive me for writing this long letter—I didn't have time to write a short one." Follow his 18th-century lead by using the techniques suggested here to capture the interest of the time-pressed 21st-century electronic user.

Most computer screens allow around 300 words before the "turn," where the reader has to scroll down. Bear this in mind as a maximum length for an email, and keep to lower limits for phone and Blackberry usage. You could also set your computer with a short screen width (known as "measure"). Screens are generally wider than writing paper and cards, so don't strain your reader's attention with endless lines that take hours to finish.

Consider how you write your e-mail: brief sentences always work best. A length of 30 words for an email sentence is usually long enough. Similarly, keep paragraphs short, with clear line spaces between them. One- or two-sentence paragraphs per key point are fine, particularly if you are asking questions. It can be helpful to use bullet points to break up a longer message so it reads more smoothly.

Humor, particularly irony, may not work well on a text or email. Messages are usually short, and without body language or tone of voice to guide

the recipient, you may find yourself misunderstood —or worse, causing grave offense when the opposite of your meaning is taken as entirely sincere. Be wary of irony, and remember that no lady or gentleman would ever use sarcasm at any time. Unless you are writing a very personal email to a trusted friend, steer clear of dramatic emotions or "heavy" feelings. Professional correspondents will be surprised—not in a good way—and others may be thrown off-balance by the directness of your language.

Don't be a bandwidth bandit—either at work or at play, always check that your recipient has the time, capacity, and desire to receive huge attachments, such as photographs or reports, or long, forwarded, illustrated emails.

Finally, stay aware of privacy and security. Your emails, texts, and forum posts can be sent on to everyone you know at the touch of a button— along with your reputation.

private emails

Consider your medium before you go online. You can use a letter, a handmade card, a cell screen and an email to wish a friend Happy Birthday—but which would you prefer to receive on your special day? Stick to snail mail to mark significant personal events, such as weddings, birthdays, and baby namings. Physical evidence—such as a beautifully printed invitation, a baby's handprint, or a carefully written formal request, add an extra level of honor to occasions and show courtesy to others.

If you're not sure whether a text or email will replace a physical letter, most etiquette experts will advise you that for personal matters, they won't. But if you are very pushed for time, a text or hasty electronic one-liner is infinitely better than no thanks at all.

And the joy of email is that, ironically, many more of us are writing letters than we used to— while in the 19th century friends always communicated by letter, the ease and speed of 21st-century technology means busy girls are eschewing the phone and returning to missives and chatty updates by mail. So, to keep up with friends, update family, and to maintain contact with distant pals, email away—the more the better.

There are 2 million emails sent every second. About 70% of these are spam, and the genuine emails are sent by around 1.3 billion email users.

business communication

Memos, letters, and even phone messages are all part of the past in our working lives—now replaced by emails, texts, and the occasional fax. But just because electronic communications have taken over snail mail, do not think old-style manners have died with them—on the contrary, courtesy, empathy, and respect are seen as more important professional attributes than ever.

As many of us now build professional relationships with people we may never meet, your texts, faxes, and emails become an ever more important part of your career standing. And as emails are easy to forward, copy, and distribute, your communications will reach a larger audience than a memo or letter ever did. All written communications at work are now vital to your personal professional brand—treat them, and your reader, with respect, and they will reward you.

Before you start tapping away in a hasty response to the ever-faster world of your working day, take a moment to consider whether you are using the right medium. Email is useful because it provides permanent, binding proof of business dealings—and it can be as formal or informal as you like. But in some matters, personal relationships still matter—so if the project or task is delicate, or you need an answer fast, you might be better off calling for a conversation, and following up by email. You need to make sure that your memos get your message across.

professional email presentation

Just as you might pick petal-strewn silk paper for a love letter, or crisp engraved white card for a cocktail party, so the presentation of your emails at work matters too. You can't—and don't need—to consider paper or handwriting, but you can make the most of simple, speedy techniques to make sure your email is every bit as professionally impressive as your best "dress for success" outfit.

Once you have composed the first draft, store your email and take time to re-read and refine it for clarity before you send it. Just because email delivery is fast, don't feel your writing has to be. Use this checklist opposite to make sure you are getting your points across with the clarity they deserve.

email checklist

- Have you filled in the subject line? If not, your email may be rejected as spam.
- Is the main point or any urgent information at the top of the email? Group headings to organize your thoughts.
- Are your sentences short and snappy? If you can cut a line or a sentence, do so—your reader will thank you for being ruthless.
- Is the email about only one subject? If you are dealing with several projects, you might find that sending one email per subject is more effective. Your recipient can file them more efficiently, and you may find separate answers more helpful.
- Have you included plenty of white space to make the email easy on the eye?

- Are the main points each given their own paragraph for clarity?
- Could you use numbered lists or bullet points to make it easier to read?
- Are the typeface and font clear? A sans-serif font ranging from 11-12 point and black type will make text simpler to read.
- Have you addressed all the points from the original email? If not, always acknowledge their receipt and note when you will reply in full.
- Are you replying to a series of questions within a long email? You can include brief "yes" and "nos" within the body of the original message for clarity. Otherwise, don't send strings or whole email histories back and forth endlessly.

dos and don'ts of emails at work

Do study the email habits of your boss and the directors to get an idea of the right tone to use. Levels of liberalism vary tremendously from firm to firm, and there is no right or wrong—so take your direction from trusted senior colleagues. And, while you may address them differently, always be as courteous in writing to the mailroom attendant as you are to the CEO.

Do avoid using emotional language, sentimentality, and strong words.

Do make sure recipients are aware of the chain of correspondence by referring to it, not including it. Similarly, never forward spam or frivolous emails without checking first.

Do keep it short and sweet—your email is a business document, not leisure reading.

Do summarize any requests at the end and include a simple electronic signature that incorporates your phone number.

Don't act in haste, repent at leisure. Save important emails and review them overnight; and never hit "Reply" in anger or without checking the facts.

Don't type in ALL CAPITALS—it is the equivalent of bad-tempered yelling in the workplace and considered rude.

Don't add off-topic remarks or repeat comments if you are joining an email discussion in order to hijack the discussion for your own ends.

Don't send very private, confidential, or secure information by email unless you are sure that both your system and the recipient's server are secure. Use passwords and change them often. Remember that for business email accounts and servers, the firm owns all of your email messages.

Don't copy in everyone in the firm unless absolutely necessary—it will annoy them. Stick to cc-ing the minimum number of colleagues.

why tact matters…

In some ways, good manners matter far more in an email than an old-fashioned letter because an email has a greater likelihood of reaching a greater number of readers. Don't forget your email may be more widely read than you think—in the modern world of work, a safe and indiscreet email does not exist.

Take the example of the Washington-based CEO of a US-wide corporation, who emailed the local manager of a regional branch in Paris, France, after a visit. The communication simply read: "Your parking lot is almost empty at 8 am; and again by 4 pm. You are my staff and you either don't know or don't care what your employees are up to—if anything. You clearly have some issues. Fix them or I will fix you." Mysteriously, the email flew round the company. On the day it was eventually posted online, the company's stock price fell by 20 percent.

At work, you will spend on average at least 49 minutes per day managing your email.

Sample emails

These examples provide guidance on the right and wrong ways to write an email.

To: <Jacob.Jones@handmadecandy.com>
From: Fiona Fudge, Confectionery Controler, Carmel's Caramels <fiona.fudge@carmelscaramels.com>
[your title settings should show the recipient your name, job title, and firm name as well as your email address]
Date: March 1, 2012 *[settings should show the date in international format, i.e., month in letters, day, year]*
Subject: Confectionery order: April 2012: our ref 1234 *[subject and purpose are clear]*

Dear Jacob *[always include a salutation—"Dear" is the usual form, but most people accept "Hi" or "Hello," too]*

I would like to place an order from you for the following supplies, which we have picked from the "handmade" section of your Spring catalog:

o   10 miniature pink-foiled Swiss chocolate doves
o   10 standard-size silver-foiled praline swallows
o   14 lemon-sugar daffodils
o   14 orange-sugar narcissi
o   8 mint-fudge grass clusters
o   1 Parma-violet sugar bouquet with licorice stems
o   32 tissue-wrapped ("in nest") fudge-centered chicks
[include key information in first line; note use of bullets to clarify details]

I would also like to confirm our monthly repeat order of:

o   48 medium sugar mice, in assorted pastel shades

I would be grateful if all the goods could be delivered to the regular address by Monday, April 2. *[use separate paragraphs to highlight other key points]*

Our order number is 1234. Please include this in your invoice. *[keep sentences short as possible]*

We are thrilled that your multicolored mice are selling so well—our younger customers seem to appreciate them while their parents browse our new salt-and-sweet caramels and dark chocolates. Do let me know if you need any more supplies of the "Midnight Treat" for your store. *[note friendly, but focused text—you are giving marketing feedback and asking for a repeat order, but not prioritizing this information]*

Don't hesitate to get in touch with me on the number below if you have any questions. *[always provide a way to reply, and contact details in your email signature]*

With all best wishes and thanks,

Regards, *[an informal sign-off is acceptable]*

Fiona Fudge
Confectionery Controler
Carmel's Caramels
212-123-4567

[for businesses, include an email disclaimer, as below]

This email and any attachments are confidential. It is intended solely for the use of the individual(s) to whom it is addressed. The views or opinions expressed are solely those of the author or sender and may not represent those of *[name of your business]*.

If you are not the intended recipient of this email, you must not copy or show it to anyone. Please contact the sender if you have received this email in error.

WHAT *NOT* TO WRITE

*In this example, the features
that others might find an irritation
are highlighted.*

To: <Jacob.Jones@handmadecandy.com>

From: <fiona@iheartbritney.com> *[personal email server—Jacob can't tell who Fiona is]*

Date: 3.1.12 *[this form of date is ambiguous to many—March 1 or 3 January?]*

Subject: Candy *[subject line too vague—Fiona does not capture attention and her email may be automatically classified as spam]*

[no salutation—many people find this impolite]

I have emailed you twice already today and have you have received it. *[chasing is inappropriate after such a short time—and a combination of bad grammar and aggression, albeit unintended, is never advisable]* I need to order your daffodils, narcissi, doves, swallows. *[order details are incomplete and cannot be processed]* Pls can you expedite this as order is urgent and our Easter display is taking place within our retail facility tomorrow. *[over-formal language sounds officious and rather rude; also, given this is a rush job, this information should be at the top]* Also 32 chicks. *[do not use abbreviated style—keep to full sentences; also, this should be above, with the rest of the stock order; keep all details that belong together in a single group, then break up paragraphs]*

Our new catalog is attached [30mb] *[a huge attachment could crash Joe's system]* 4U *[avoid texting jargon]*

[no sign-off or thanks increases risk of causing offense]

Fona *[always proofread an email before you send it—incorrectly spelling your own name will never give a good impression]*

[no contact details]

PS and the mice *[unclear—is Fiona a pest control officer? Who can tell?]*

SOCIAL NETWORKING
chatting online

While the modern trend to liberalism and generous information-sharing pulls us one way, and can be great fun, the realization that our line manager might see a startling underwear-clad party portrait pulls us the other—which is why blogging, chat sites, and social networking sites need rules too; even tech savvy users need to set boundaries. Although many forums are intimate or informal, unwary users will be reminded with the curtness of Emily Post if they break the rules, so advice for newbies is here, too.

starting out online

Blogs, forums, walls, and chat rooms—what's not to love? Surely the only problem is thinking up a killer line…? Well, not quite. While you may wish to devastate friends with your wit, the novice user may find themselves causing a quite different effect—many sites are a minefield of potential offense. Many social sites have complicated etiquette, and while we have no business here with the specifics, the rules below will give you a grounding in online manners ideal for the social networking debutante—and tips for her elder, more worldly sister too.

When you've found a forum or chat room that interests you, "lurk"—that is, observe—before posting. Read various discussions, check profiles, and absorb the tone and level of informality of experienced users. Also, read the site's own FAQs (frequently asked questions), user rules, or house guide before you draft your first comment.

With many of these websites, you will be given the opportunity to create a "profile"—a page with selected information about yourself. It's fine to include your birth date, but not your birth year, for security reasons. Similarly, take advantage of the privacy settings—don't be afraid to reveal your interests and hobbies, but steer clear of revealing more personal details. Be selective about what else you reveal in your profile—advertisers may take advantage: for instance, if you include your "relationship status" as "engaged," be prepared for a bombardment of ads for flowers, cakes, dresses, and even flower girls for hire. Finally, don't boast on your profile—as with a "glorified" resume, you may be found out.

post guidelines

Before you post anything, always announce yourself as a newbie—users will be more tolerant of errors, and will be keen to give you the benefit of their site wisdom. In theory, you can post whatever you like—but take care not to irritate regular users. Many old-timers on sites consider discussions their personal property, and flame the unwary for simply holding a different view. Do not retaliate or begin a "flame war."

Also, stay on the topic. For instance, asking for advice about where to buy the latest Louboutin glitter pumps on a "Make Do and Mend" crafting site is not a good idea. Equally, don't "troll"—post a deliberately provocative thread or question to see what response you might get. Apart from ruining the integrity of genuine discussion, you will be easily spotted and probably banned.

photos

Sharing photos online has become a huge part of many people's internet experience, but exercise a little caution. Don't post an unduly flattering self-portrait. No one wants to be told, "You look better online." Equally, avoid obviously provocative or revealing shots unless you wish to be approached by the desperate (you don't). Bear in mind that you want to avoid blurring the lines of your professional and personal life—a single "hilarious" photo may not be worth any conclusions it draws.

Just as you would be circumspect post-party about posting a particularly fetching portrait of yourself covered in shaving cream, do not feel it is acceptable to post the snapshot of your best friend wearing only a balloon. Respect others' privacy as you would your own.

separate web and work personas

Web experts claim that our individual web history will become one of our most important personal issues. Already, employment law courts are dealing with cases where employees have been fired for posting inappropriate personal material about themselves online. The cases reached court regardless of the fact the workers involved had posted photos and messages about their group of friends in their own time—and nothing posted commented directly on the reputation of the company. Unfortunately, the web means that the personal cannot remain private once it is online, as many disgruntled employees are finding to their cost.

The lesson here is to show yourself good manners—keep your social web personality and your professional standing separate. If you're not sure what is inappropriate, dull as it may be, err on the safe side. As a simple test, ask yourself how you would feel if your mother or manager saw the material in a newspaper.

making friends

Web forums and chat rooms provide a way of meeting people that is relatively easy. People tend to make new friends via work or social activities, while online, you need not leave the

comfort of your living room. However, keep in mind the anonymity online correspondence brings and be careful about what details you reveal about yourself. Take your time in interacting with other web users, and do not introduce yourself to all and sundry—respected British etiquette authority Debrett's declares that accumulating "friends" is "not a competition."

While you may accumulate many friends—the Facebook average currently numbers 170—do not delight your entire address book with every message. In the age of endless messaging, remember—less is more. Targeting your communications will keep everyone interested.

When posting, avoid "eek-mail." Sitting behind a computer screen offers a certain freedom that you don't get when talking face-to-face, but keep it under control: don't post soul-baring screeds unless you don't mind your boss or bank manager reading it. In the same way, you might read something you didn't need or want to know; stalking, or checking the profiles of former love interests, usually turns out to be depressing.

Finally, learn to turn the computer off, and stay connected to the outside world, too.

text etiquette

After fifteen years of texting, one would have thought that the rules of SMS would be clear, but many of us still find the humble text message a social hurdle. Ironically, PDAs and cell phones have greatly improved our manners—it's now no problem to inform a friend we will be moments late, or to acknowledge a last-minute invitation with a promptness that would leave Emily Post dumbstruck. Cell phones can keep us in touch, improve our friendliness, and allow us to fulfil

the seven golden rules of social networking

There is no higher form of good manners than assisting the inexperienced. As a regular on your favorite site, show your skill by using these tips, then pass them on to newbies to make them feel at home:

1. Acknowledge important messages and invitations as soon as you receive them. Debrett's advises that a delay of a day is acceptable before answering an invitation, but do acknowledge it in the meantime.
2. Don't "flame" anyone—your criticism can turn into an unedifying row that will certainly not show you at your best.
3. Keep messages neat and sweet—don't be brief for the sake of it, but remember your reader's attention span. Warn other users about long posts, and use short lines, succinct paragraphs, and plenty of white space to increase the chances of your post being read.
4. Be wary of what you upload: Never upload anything you haven't viewed yourself or any stolen material or art—photos, music, or film—that belongs to someone else without asking first, and don't upload large files or attachments without checking that the site and other users want them.
5. Include your email address (if appropriate), but keep other people's email addresses to yourself unless specifically allowed to pass them on.
6. Keep feelings light, bright, and easy unless you know everyone well, and don't be lured by speed and convenience into posting an oh-so-sharp quip that may backfire.
7. Keep to the thread topic. If you want to start a discussion, do so on a new thread, not by posting on another user's discussion.

our social duties all the better; but, as with the speed and convenience of email, pitfalls await the unwary.

Similar to forum chat and email, the speed of the medium can lead us into sending unwise communications and declarations. The ever-present nature of the cell or mobile phone can lead us into causing accidental offense—is it appropriate to read a long message from a faraway friend at a dinner party? Equally, the informality of the medium can cause problems: how do you address your manager or a web-wizard great aunt? As with other correspondence, the basics of etiquette—that is, simple courtesy and consideration—still apply.

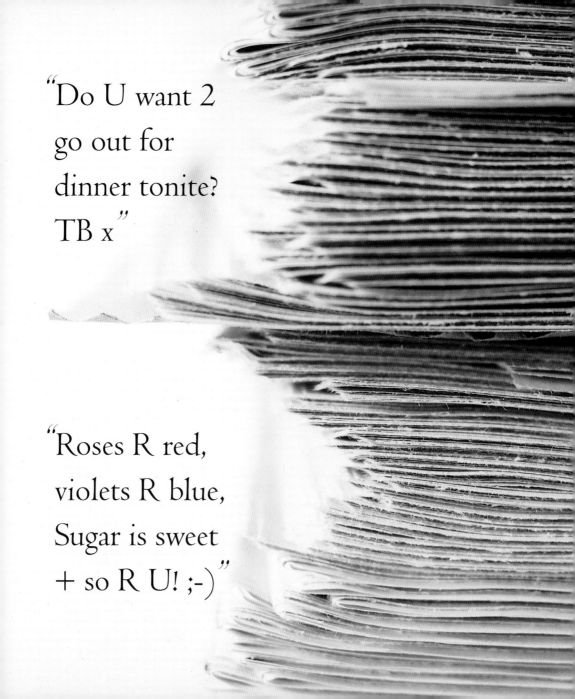

"Do U want 2 go out for dinner tonite? TB x"

"Roses R red, violets R blue, Sugar is sweet + so R U! ;-)"

texting dos and don'ts

DO practice safe text. Be aware that however harmless those short lines seem to you, your public standing travels with them. Keep deeply emotional, sweary, saucy, or private texts within a small circle of friends.

DO check and double-check the name of the recipient. Texts that go astray can be awkward for everyone.

DO respect others' privacy. Delete strong texts from close friends, and never forward indiscreet messages.

DO avoid abbreviations and text slang when dealing with the elderly or colleagues at work. Write professional messages and family texts with complete words and sentences, keeping them (necessarily) brief.

DO avoid irony—however funny and kind you are trying to be, the lack of a voice means your joke may not work. Even a simple phrase—"How buff did you look at the BBQ?"—may backfire.

DON'T send invitations to a formal event, such as a christening or bat mitzvah, by text. Your guests may lose it, and will require more information than their phones or PDAs can handle.

DON'T read—or worse, send—messages when you are in a meeting or out with a group of friends (unless you suspect an emergency). Texting another when you are in conversation is as impolite as making a long phone call.

DON'T send clusters of photos or music unless the recipient has asked for them in advance.

DON'T chase the recipient for a reply. They may be busy or, heaven forbid, their phone may be off. Respect others' privacy and right to downtime.

DON'T text late at night or in the early morning—it might wake—or worse, frighten—the recipient.

acronyms

Confused by what the text you've just received actually means? This little guide should help.

BBFN = Bye bye for now
BTW = By the way
IMHO = In my humble opinion
IYKWIM = If you know what I mean
LOL = Laughing out loud
NP = No problem
NNTR = No need to reply
ROTFL = Rolling on the floor laughing
TB = Text back
TTFN = Ta ta for now
WBS = Write back soon

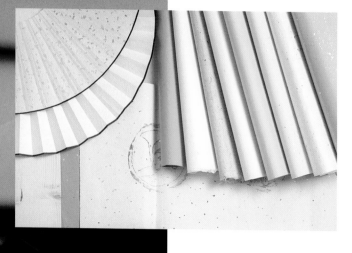

CHAPTER 5

The Finishing Touch

Paper and pens are the shoes and handbags of your writing style—you and your message deserve to get them right. This section suggests a variety of paper styles you can choose from, and explains how to choose a pen that feels right. If you want to be truly individual, you will find out how to make your own paper for invitations. And to complete the perfect presentation of your letter, follow this guide to addressing envelopes and using correct titles and salutations.

PERFECT PAPER & PENS
choose with care

Picking out the creamiest, silkiest paper for your letter, and using the smoothest pen, is one of the most delicious pleasures of letter-writing. A small but sensual joy for you and your recipient, your choice matters because it shows respect (nothing frivolous about that) to you both, and honors your words and their attention. Advice is offered here on what stationery you might choose, and you will also find a guide on how to store your correspondence, using tips and tricks from museums.

stylish stationery

Unlike the diktats of etiquette, which can seem a chore, or the painstaking journey to self-expression in a love letter, creating your personal letter presentation style should be nothing but an easy enjoyment you should take time to savor. Writers have always known the importance of creating an individual frame for their private words—among her few possessions, Jane Austen owned a tiny oak writing desk, filled with pure white, almost translucent, sheets of feather-light paper and a tiny pot of jet black ink, to relay her innermost thoughts to her beloved family.

Carried everywhere she went, one can't help thinking she knew how important, and how delightful, her style of communication was.

Whether you like thick, rich engraved card stock and blue-black ink from a heavy, walnut fountain pen, fuchsia postcards and gold ink, or blossom-strewn handmade paper overlaid with drifting watercolor, take time to choose your own letter style. Good stationery should be as chic as you are, and your mail-ready letter should make you feel as good as the moment you are ready to go out for a special evening.

types of paper

Museums of the world showcase their earliest precious paper displays, some dating back thousands of years, whether they form a significant contribution to a long-lost civilization or, more likely, are still part of our cultural treasure chest today. From the earliest examples where paper was first invented—inked Chinese manuscripts kept in rolls from 5,000 BCE—to cracked, spindly declarations of love on rough 18th-century scraps kept carefully by a famous poet's first love, paper matters.

Choose one of the following special papers so that your letter will reflect the care and attention you will give to writing it. It will also ensure that it will last for as long as the recipient wishes to keep it.

classic papers

These papers are always a good choice and are readily available.

o   **Florentine writing paper, usually sold by weight (known as a quire)**

o   **Watercolor paper, which gives a slightly rough texture**

o   **Marbled paper**—the best is Italian and handmade, but you can easily make your own with watercolor paper and ink

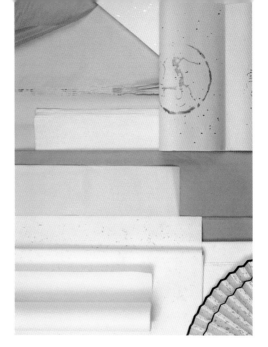

well brought-up and British

For traditional forms of correspondence, you may want to adopt a similarly traditional style of paper.

o   **Surprisingly thick cartridge paper**—the thicker your ink, the thicker the paper should be. Buy it in an "art block" of 10 or 20 sheets.

o   **Your writing paper should be engraved (not printed) with your address at the top, centered in blue or black serif 18th-century type.**

o   **Acceptable colors are white, cream, and gray-blue.**

o   **If you have stationery made, include only your name on postcards.**

eastern-style papers

Make your letter stand out with paper from faraway places.

o Chinese: handmade "parchment" look, sprinkled with gold inclusions or silver flecks

o Chinese: yuanshu or mao bian paper, known as grass or rice paper (actually made of bamboo)

o Japanese: fine but pliable sheets of paper with silk fibers

o Japanese: handmade and handmilled paper with rough fibers

o Japanese: chiyogami, or printed origami paper

craft papers

Many mainstream stores now offer alternatives to standard writing paper; look for paper with inclusions that may include:

o Dried blooms and blossoms, leaves and stems

o Shreds of sparkling fibers or metallics

o Rags or textiles

o Recycled inclusions

Finally, of course, don't forget the all-important scrap paper for first drafts. You can use anything, and it makes eco-sense to reuse as much discarded business correspondence and junk mail as possible.

choosing a pen

Nothing beats the feel of writing with a heavy, solid ink pen. Apart from adding weight to your words and providing a slick but serious  impression, ink pens come with a range of nibs, one of which will really suit you. Try a flat, chisel-edged nib or a very fine nib to find out which is most comfortable for you— no small consideration when planning a lifetime of correspondence. If you want to use a particular ink, choose a fountain pen with a refillable reservoir—otherwise you can stick to cartridge pens, which take ready-made, slightly more watery, ink.

storing your letters

Your letters need protecting to survive—rather like one's complexion, they need to be guarded from excesses of temperature and atmosphere. Don't store letters at the top or bottom of the house—the attic will probably be too warm, while the basement will be too cold and may be damp. Use a tin box to protect your letters. You can keep letters in their envelopes, but make sure nothing is damp or dirty before it is wrapped. Tie precious bundles in date order with silk or velvet ribbon, and wrap parcels in acid-free tissue paper. Store them loosely stacked. As a finale, sprinkle dried lavender, rosebuds, or pot pourri into the container—whenever you open the tin box, you will relive your most precious memories in a scented cloud of flowers.

ADDRESSING AN ENVELOPE
the pièce de résistance

Although for us, the envelope is the last stage of correspondence, for the recipient, it creates the vital first impression. So a correctly addressed envelope is not just an afterthought—it needs to be as elegant as its contents. Luckily, this is relatively simple—only a few points will create your final flourish.

envelope etiquette

An easy way to make a good impression is to use matching paper and envelopes. A 10-inch (22.5-cm) or Monarch envelope is ideal for personal correspondence, while business letters tend to use 10-inch ones only. If you are striking a traditional note, handwrite your envelope in black, blue, or blue-black ink. Otherwise, match the ink to the letter.

No matter how informal the contents of the letter, use a complete, formal name and address on the envelope. Position the first line of the address in the horizontal center of the address, and slightly below the vertical center. Indent each line by two letter spaces as you work down the address, or keep the whole name address flush left (see pages 151–2 for templates demonstrating this). In the US, it is good form to also include your own name and address in the top-left-hand corner.

You should either use punctuation throughout, or leave it out (except for titles such as Mr., Mrs., Miss., Ms., etc.). Only use abbreviations such as "St." for street, "Ave." for avenue, and "Rd." for road if you are short of space, and if you do, use them consistently. Capitalize names of people, roads, and places, cities, states, and countries.

See page 23 and the title directory (pages 153–156) to avoid the etiquette minefield of modern coupledom and for ways to address the great and the good, including politicians and the clergy. If you are writing to an entire family, you should address them as "the Brookfields" (not "the Brookfields'," which is possessive rather than plural.)

If you're sending out invitations, enclose them and any response cards in size order, with the most important uppermost. Put the main invitation on top so that it can be seen immediately when the envelope is opened. As a final courteous touch, make sure any RSVP cards are stamped.

A Formal Envelope

These examples show various ways in which you can address an envelope formally.

Ms. F. G. Harris,
1, Yellow Cat Rd.,
Pawtown, CA 12345,
USA

Mr. and Mrs. C.A.R. Harris,
25, Blue Sky Way,
Happytown, C.A. 12345,
USA

Ms. FG Harris
1 Yellow Cat Rd
Pawtown, C.A. 12345
USA

MODERN ADDRESS STYLES
*Alternative, and more
modern, address forms
use neither punctuation
nor indentation.*

Mr. and Mrs. CAR Harris
25 Blue Sky Way
Happytown, C.A. 12345
USA

directory of titles and salutations

Unlikely as it seems that you could end up as pen pals with royalty, an archbishop, senator, or various members of the peerage, don't rule it out. Be prepared with this directory in case you need to get in touch with any illuminati in public life (and see page 157 for further reading on the subject).

Remember to add any decorations to the envelope—not jaunty stickers and sparkle clusters, but military decorations and honorifics; royalty and many senior peers, including women, have them. List them in order of importance.

Tip: The British spelling of honour and honourable contains a **"u"**; if you are writing from the US, keep the British version for a British title.

writing to royalty

Don't start the letter with **"Dear"**—a simple **"Your …"** is enough. And should your letter succeed in getting you an audience with the royal person, once the introductions are over, you should address princes and royal dukes as **"Sir,"** and female members of royalty as **"Ma'am"** (to rhyme with ham).

THE QUEEN

On the envelope: **HM The Queen**
Salutation: **Your Majesty**
Throughout the letter: **Your Majesty**

THE PRINCE OF WALES

On the envelope: **HRH The Prince of Wales**
Salutation: **Your Royal Highness**
Throughout the letter: **Your Royal Highness**

WIFE OF THE PRINCE OF WALES

On the envelope: **HRH The Duchess of Cornwall**
Salutation: **Your Royal Highness**
Throughout the letter: **Your Royal Highness**

ROYAL DUKE

On the envelope: **HRH The Duke of York**
Salutation: **Your Royal Highness**
Throughout the letter: **Your Royal Highness**

writing to a peer

Many forms of address exist, but only the main ones are included here. There are five types of peer that run in descending order: dukes, marquesses, earls, viscounts, and barons. Use **"The Right Honourable"** only where the peer is a member of the Privy Council.

DUKES:

On the envelope: **His Grace The Duke of Cake**
Salutation: **My Lord Duke** or **Your Grace**

DUCHESS

On the envelope: **Her Grace The Duchess of Cake**
On the envelope: **Dear Duchess** or **Your Grace**

MARQUESS OR MARQUIS

On the envelope: **The Most Hon. The Marquess of Meringue**
Salutation: **My Lord Marquess, Dear Lord Meringue** or **Your Lordship**

MARCHIONESS

On the envelope: **The Most Hon. The Marchioness of Meringue**
Salutation: **Madam** or **Dear Lady Meringue**

EARL

On the envelope: **The Rt. Hon. The Earl Grey**
Salutation: **My Lord** or **Dear Lord Grey**

COUNTESS

On the envelope: **The Rt. Hon. The Countess Eclair**
Salutation: **Madam** or **Dear Lady Eclair**

VISCOUNT

On the envelope: **The Rt. Hon. The Viscount Cupcake**
Salutation: **My Lord** or **Dear Lord Cupcake**

VISCOUNTESS

On the envelope: **The Rt. Hon. The Viscountess Cupcake**
Salutation: **Madam** or **Dear Lady Cupcake**

BARONESS (in her own right)

On the envelope: **The Rt. Hon. The Lady Lemon-tart** or **The Rt. Hon. The Baroness Lemon-tart**
Salutation: **Madam** or **Dear Lady Lemon-tart**

BARON

On the envelope: **The Rt. Hon. The Lord Shortbread**
Salutation: **My Lord** or **Dear Lord Shortbread**

BARONESS (married to a baron, i.e., the title is her husband's right)

On the envelope: **The Rt. Hon. The Lady Shortbread**
Salutation: **Dear Lady Shortbread (not Baroness)**

the system of titles

Eldest sons—i.e., the heirs—of dukes, marquesses, and earls use their father's highest secondary title. If a titled girl marries, she takes her husband's title, unless hers was higher in the first place. For instance, Lady Jane Spencer, the late Princess of Wales' sister, married a Sir Robert Fellowes—had she no title of her own, she would have become Lady Fellowes, but as the daughter of an earl, she is a Lady in her own right and is known as Lady Jane Fellowes. Scottish titles are slightly different—if they have no other title, Scottish heirs use "Master" and "Mistress."

Only the wife of a peer receives "The" before the title— for instance: Her Grace the Duchess of Marlborough; the honorific is not used for the wife of a baronet or a knight. The first name of a Lady is generally not used in correspondence unless she is titled in her own right. For example, Lady Elodie Lafosse would signify a girl who is the daughter of a duke, or an earl, whereas Lady Lafosse is the correct form for a Lady who has married her title. If a man marries a titled lady, he does not acquire her title.

writing to the gentry

Take care to use the correct form of address and salutation to avoid offense when writing a letter to a member of the gentry.

BARONETS

On the envelope: **Sir Oliver Savory, Bt.**
Salutation: **Dear Sir Oliver**

BARONET'S WIFE

On the envelope: **Lady Savory**
Salutation: **Dear Lady Savory**

DAME

On the envelope: **Dame Joan Toast, Btss.**
Salutation: **Dear Dame Joan**

KNIGHTS

On the envelope: **Sir James Jam**
Salutation: **Dear Sir James**

A SCOTTISH CLAN CHIEF

The exact style of each Scottish chief's title is based on family tradition rather than a set system; however, these guidelines are a start.

On the envelope (but check first): **Chief Oatcake of Oatcake, Iain Oatcake of Edinburgh, Iain Oatcake of that Ilk, The Oatcake of Perth, The Oatcake of Oatcake, or The Oatcake**

Salutation: **Sir** should do the trick, but check.

A SCOTTISH LAIRD

On the envelope: **The Much Honoured Tom Thistle of Harris** or **The Much Honoured The Laird of Harris**
Salutation: **Sir** or **Dear Laird Tom Thistle** or **Dear Laird Harris**

THE WIFE OF A LAIRD

On the envelope: **The Much Honoured Flora Bird of Skye** or **The Much Honoured The Lady of Skye**
Salutation: **Madam** or **Dear Lady Skye**

writing to the clergy

Follow these guidelines for letters to members of the clergy.

RABBI

On the envelope: **Rabbi Gene Blue** or **Rabbi Blue**
Salutation: **Dear Rabbi** or **Dear Rabbi Blue**

ARCHBISHOP

On the envelope: **The Most Rev. and Rt. Hon. The Lord Archbishop of Canterbury** (or, if not in Privy Council, **The Most Rev. Oliver Pickles**)
Salutation: **Dear Archbishop** or **Your Grace**

BISHOP

On the envelope: **The Rt. Rev. and Rt. Hon. The Lord Bishop of Royal Tunbridge Wells**
Salutation: **Dear Bishop** or **My Lord**

VICAR

On the envelope: **The Rev. Anna Orange**
Salutation: **Dear Mr./Mrs./Ms Orange**

PRIEST

On the envelope: **Father Anthony Tate**
Salutation: **Dear Father Tate** or **Dear Father Anthony**

politicians

Write to British cabinet ministers with their proper titles:

PRIME MINISTER

On the envelope: **The Right Honourable The Prime Minister and First Lord of the Treasury**
Salutation: **Dear Prime Minister**

DEPUTY PRIME MINISTER

On the envelope: **The Right Honourable The Deputy Prime Minister and First Secretary of State**
Salutation: **Dear Deputy Prime Minister**

CHANCELLOR OF THE EXCHEQUER

On the envelope: **The Right Honourable The Chancellor of the Exchequer**
Salutation: **Dear Chancellor**

LORD CHANCELLOR

On the envelope: **The Right Honourable The Lord Chancellor and Secretary of State for Justice**
Salutation: **Dear Lord Chancellor**

For the rest of the government, use ministers' personal names:

On the envelope: **Sam Smalley Esq. MP Minister of State, Department of Health Minister**
Salutation: **Dear Minister**

senators and representatives

Just as with politicians, when writing to senators and representatives, make sure you use the correct form of address.

SENATOR

On the envelope:
The Honorable Fred Harris
United States Senate
Washington, D.C. 20510
Salutation: **Dear Senator Harris**

CHAIRPERSON OF A COMMITTEE OR THE SPEAKER OF THE HOUSE

On the envelope:
The Honorable Stanley Ray
Chairman, Committee on Health
Health Committee
United States Senate
Washington, D.C. 20510
Salutation: **Dear Mr. Chairman, Dear Madam Chairwoman, Dear Mr. Speaker, Dear Madam Speaker**

U.S. SUPREME COURT

Address your congressman as you would a senator. Then identify the bill you are writing about—use the Thomas Legislative Information System to find the number. You will need a number for:

o   House Bills, House Resolutions, and House Joint Resolution
o   Senate Bills, Senate Resolutions, and Senate Joint Resolutions

resources

further reading on etiquette

US: The U.S. Capitol Switchboard at (202) 224-3121 will help you and connect you to the Senate office you need.

The Senate website lists all Senators, with their capitol addresses and a link to their own Senate website, that gives addresses for their state offices and telephone numbers. You can also email Senators through a link on the site.

UK: The use of titles is a complex subject and we advise you to check one of these sources for individual details of the names and customs of the peerage. If any doubt remains, you should contact the UK Government's Crown Office.

Debrett's Correct Form (Headline, 1999)
Useful guide that explains how to address professionals, academics, the military and diplomats, British lawyers, local government officials the clergy, the peerage, and the royal family.

Titles and forms of address: a guide to correct use (21st ed.) (A&C Black, 2002)
Traditional source of how to address letters and formal invitations to a range of people from peers to judges, bishops to professors, both men and women, and their spouses. There is also advice on addressing them in speech and pronouncing the more unusual surnames and titles.

Whitaker's Almanack
Published annually, this guide contains references to different groups, with an updated list of baronets and knights.

Crockford's Guide to Addressing the Clergy.
Now available online, this guide explains how to write to and address members of the Anglican Church
http://www.crockford.org.uk/standard.asp?id=116

useful addresses

SMYTHSON
40 New Bond Street
London, W1S 2DE
Tel: + 44 (0)20 7629 8558
www.smythson.com

Smythson offers swanky stationery, used by the English Royal Family, and most international celebrities. Known for its collaborations with the new wave of international fashion designers, the store also provides you with the best and most luxurious traditional stationery.

THE WREN PRESS (US)
Madison Avenue, 10th Floor
57th Street
New York, NY 10022
Tel: +1 (212) 832 7011
Email:
ann.patron@wrenpress.com
www.wrenpress.co.uk/x/us/default.html?changeregion=1

THE WREN PRESS (UK)
1 Chelsea Wharf
15 Lots Road
London, SW10 0QJ
Tel: +44 (0)20 7351 5887
www.wrenpress.co.uk

The Wren Press has been praised by *Vogue's* Secret Address Book as "One of the UK's most trusted stationers." Supplies engraved stationery worldwide.

SELFRIDGES
Selfridges London
400 Oxford Street
London, W1A 1AB
Tel: (from abroad) + 44 (0) 113 369 8040
Tel: (from UK) 0800 123 400

Selfridges provides smart society papers and pens.

FRANCESCO PINEIDER SpA
Via Industriale, 12
25014 Castenedolo (BS)
Tel: +39 030 2130172
Email:
info@pineidershop.com
www.pineidershop.com

Trading since 1774, this Italian store sells beautiful Florentine marbled paper.

index

acknowledgments

PHOTOGRAPHY CREDITS

CAROLINE ARBER
Pages 34: designed and made by Jane
Cassini and Ann Brownfield, 70-71,
81: designed and made by Jane
Cassini and Ann Brownfield, 146

CAROLYN BARBER
Pages 6, 58

DAN DUCHARS
Page 127:
www.hogartharchitects.co.uk

DANIEL FARMER
Page 97

WINFRIED HEINZE
Pages 5, 48, 122-123 main

JANINE HOSEGOOD
Page 45

SANDRA LANE
Page 1, 27, 49, 93, 104-105 main

TOM LEIGHTON
Pages 112-113 background

DAVID LOFTUS
Page 37

DAVID MONTGOMERY
Page 148

KRISTIN PERERS
Page 91

CLAIRE RICHARDSON
Pages 61, 137

DEBI TRELOAR
Pages 41, 57, 99, 136

ANDREW WOOD
Page 125

POLLY WREFORD
Pages 2-3, 15, 23, 36, 47, 55, 71
inset, 84, 86, 95, 100, 105 inset,
111, 126, 140, 142-143 main, 147,
150, 155

FOLLOWING IMAGES ALL COURTESY OF GETTY IMAGES

ph = photographer, col = collection

Page 10 ph GEORGE MARKS, col Hulton Archive
Page 38 ph GEORGE MARKS, col Retrofile
Page 43 ph GEORGE MARKS, col Retrofile RF
Page 46 ph GEORGE MARKS, col Hulton Archive
Page 53 ph N SMITH, col Hulton Archive
Page 60 ph GEORGE MARKS, col Retrofile RF
Page 64 ph JEFFREY HAMILTON, col Digital Vision
Page 68 ph FPG, col Hulton Archive
Page 72 ph GEORGE MARKS, col Hulton Archive
Page 75 ph CHRIS WINDSOR, col Stone
Page 82 ph MEL CURTIS, col Photodisc

Page 87 ph MEL CURTIS, col Photodisc
Page 90 ph ORLANDO, col Hulton Archive
Page 106 ph GENERAL PHOTOGRAPHIC AGENCY, col
    Hulton Archive
Page 116 ph JOHN SADOVY, col Hulton Archive
Pages 123 and 138 ph VLADIMIR GODNIK, col fStop
Page 124 ph H. ARMSTRONG ROBERTS, col Retrofile
Page 131 ph PHOTODISC, col Photodisc
Page 135 ph GEORGE MARKS, col Retrofile
Page 144 ph FPG, col Hulton Archive
Page 149 ph GEORGE MARKS, col Retrofile